MINISTERING ONE TO ANOTHER

HOW GOD USES THE WILLING AND OBEDIENT TO CHANGE LIVES

MARY H. JOHNSON

Copyright ©2007 by Mary H Johnson

P.O. Box 422914
Kissimmee, FL 34742-2914
or e-mail mjohnsonbos@aol.com

MINISTERING ONE TO ANOTHER
by Mary H. Johnson

Printed in the United States of America

ISBN 978-1-60266-755-6

All rights reserved solely by the author. The author guarantees all contents are original and do not infringe upon the legal rights of any other person or work. No part of this book may be reproduced in any form without the permission of the author. The views expressed in this book are not necessarily those of the publisher.

Unless otherwise indicated all scripture quotations in this book are taken from the New King James Version, Copyright © 1979, 1980, 1982. Thomas Nelson Inc. Used by permission.

Scripture quotation marked (NIV) are taken from The HOLY BIBLE, NEW INTERNATIONAL VERSION ® Copyright 1973, 1978, 1984 by International Bible Society. Used by permission of Zondervan Publishing House. All rights reserved.

Scripture quotations marked (AMP) are taken from THE AMPLIFIED BIBLE, Old Testament Copyright © 1695, 1987 by Zondervan Corporation. The Amplified New Testament copyright © 1658, 1987 by the Lockman Foundation. Used by permission.

www.xulonpress.com

863-514-5090

This book is dedicated to all believers who want to move beyond the confines of traditional concepts of ministry into the unlimited power of the Holy Spirit within them to meet the needs of others for the Glory of God.

Acknowledgements

I gratefully thank the Holy Spirit for giving me the inspiration, guidance and total provision to accomplish this project. It is a work that I pray will help many embrace their calling, understand and use their anointing in the service of others bringing Glory to God.

I am also especially thankful to the following individuals for their contribution in making this dream a reality:

Bonnie for challenging me to go forward with this book. It is amazing how we met on a flight from San Diego to Orlando and how the Lord used Bonnie to motivate me through her testimony to start writing the things the Lord had placed in my heart.

Maureen, for reminding me through a word of prophecy that the Lord had expectations of me, and that I needed to respond to the assignment He had given to me. Maureen's prayers and editorial assistance were invaluable to completing this work.

Gladys, for befriending and interceding for me; for her words of encouragement that kept me focused so I could complete this work on the time schedule.

Stewart, for his inspiration, timely prayers and communication that kept me energized from time to time during this project.

My daughter, Cassandra for her diligence, resourcefulness, continuous support, encouragement and editing assistance with this material.

TABLE OF CONTENTS

i.	Introduction - My Earliest Memories of Ministry	xi
I.	Understanding the Voice and Ways of God	17
II.	Understanding the Concept of Ministry	29
III.	Called and Chosen for Ministry	41
IV.	Responding to the Call to Ministry	51
V.	Jesus as a Model for Ministry	61
VI.	Personal Preparation for Ministry	75
VII.	Going Forth In Ministry	83
VIII.	Ministering to the Wounded	103
IX.	Persevering in Ministry	111
X.	Maintaining Your Spiritual House	127
XI.	Exalting Jesus Everywhere	133

Introduction

My Earliest Memories of Ministry

My earliest recollection of a minister and ministry dates back to my childhood. I was about seven years old, living in the British colony of Montserrat, a territory of 32 ½ square miles in area, in the beautiful Leeward Islands, planted in the Caribbean Sea. My parents were Anglicans, members of the branch of the Episcopal Church of England. We attended worship at the St. George's Parish Church, one of four such parish churches on the island.

The minister was the priest, the male spiritual leader in each church. We called him, Father followed by his last name. He wore special attire, usually in a long, black gown with a white collar and a cord belt around his waist. His attire would change on special occasions such as weddings, Holy Communion and Easter. Everyone honored the minister. He was regarded as being holy and sacred. I had never seen him in regular clothing as an ordinary man, hence I saw all priests as being close to God, very special, serving as leaders of churches and being well respected in the community. The priest preached every Sunday, served Holy Communion, conducted infant christening, weddings and funerals. This revered spiritual leader made seasonal visits to the homes of members of the parish - where he served communion to the sick. He also visited and prayed for those who were in the hospital.

The priest conducted the religious education for the children each Wednesday morning from 9:00 am to 10:00 am. All the children of Anglican parentage were required to attend the session before joining their other classmates in the public school. Confirmation was a vital part of religious education. Without it one could not participate in Communion. Confirmation was the culmination of a process in which adults or children age twelve and older successfully partook in a series of religious classes. Each class completion was marked with a ceremonial event in which the celebrants received their first Communion. Confirmation meant being made an official member of the church.

The minister also listened to confessions from individuals in the Church at scheduled times. He would pray to God for the penitent and give them passages of scripture for future reading. The scripture passages contained words of assurance that their sins were forgiven. In retrospect it seems like the burden of the ministry rested mainly on one person with some vestry help with the much lighter duties. Little did I know that Christ called us all as Christians to help in these vital duties of ministry, that His salvation and Spirit empower us for these acts and more.

At that stage of my life I knew nothing of salvation, though I was taught that Jesus was the Son of God, was born of the Virgin Mary, that He lived in this world, died and rose from the dead. I learned Jesus was seated at the right hand of the Father, and that He was coming back one day to judge the quick and the dead. I also learned of the Holy Spirit, the Catholic Church or the universal Christian Church, and that there will be a resurrection of the dead, and life in the world to come. The application of these truths in my life remained to be seen. However, it is the work of these priests that planted the seed for salvation and service to God in my heart. Later exposures and experiences with different types of ministry would show me how to apply these truths.

My First Encounters with Personal Ministry

On occasion my mother would take me shopping with her and we would see some beautiful women dressed in black or white gowns, with starchy white circular collars, and wore white special bonnets on their heads. I could clearly see their faces but not the hair. They also wore a corded belt around their waist with a Rosary hanging at the side. I was curious and yet somewhat afraid to touch these ladies. My mom explained that they were Nuns, a special people of God who prayed a lot, worshipped at the Roman Catholic Church, taught in the Catholic school and lived in the convent. Their lives were dedicated to serving God and others.

As I grew up I wanted to know more about God, and the special things about Him. I loved reading and I became interested in reading the Bible. I even memorized many of the Psalms such as: Psalms 8, 23, 91, 101, 121. Today those psalms have served as a reminder of God's greatness, provision, protection and guidance. They minister God's great love and mercy to me during tough times.

The more I read, the more my curiosity intensified. I found that there were so many stories in the Bible. I wanted to know as many as I could share with my parents and family. I was especially fascinated telling them of stories that were found only in the books of the Apocrypha.

By the time of my late adolescence, I was teaching full time in a primary school on week days and a Sunday School group of six to eight-year old children each Sunday afternoon. I had not at that time experienced a personal salvation in Jesus Christ, neither did I know how to become a partaker of His divine nature; empowering me through His Spirit to minister unto Him and serve my fellow man. I did not realize how much our Heavenly Father was drawing me to Him with strong cords of love to be a minister. He would one day declare this to me: I would not be a nun in a Catholic convent or the spiritual leader of a church, but a woman servant and a minister for Him.

After a year or so of teaching the Sunday school, I left the position to pursue other interests. The parish priest, Father Persico then summoned me to a meeting where he reprimanded me for my action. In his remarks he said: *"The Lord has a calling on your life and you are running from it"*. I was self-willed, and was not eager to retract my decision, but rather justified the behavior with an excuse that so much teaching was too much on my voice. In hind sight, I know it was pride that hindered me from submitting to the man of God. However, our God is longsuffering and merciful and does not reward us after our iniquities but patiently waits for our repentance.

I believe that Father Persico prayed for me and possibly offered the type of prayer that caused God to arrest my spirit so that one day I would discover Him and align myself with His will for my life. I believe this to be true because of the Word that says,

> *"Obey them that have rule over you, and submit yourselves: for they watch for your souls as they that must give account, that they may do it with joy, and not with grief: for that is unprofitable for you."*
> *Heb. 13:17 (KJV)*

Jesus did a similar thing for Simon Peter, one of His disciples, who was destined for a major work in the ministry and whom Satan was determined to hinder. Jesus saw it, and exposed the enemy's plans. He then prayed for Peter before He went to the cross and further admonished Peter to strengthen the brethren after regaining his strength.

You can find more in-depth information as you read the gospel according to Luke 22:31, 32.

I continued to teach in the primary education and shortly afterwards pursued a college degree in Puerto Rico. The hand of my God followed me to college. My roommate was a Christian young lady— Seventh Day Adventist. Of course, the University's Housing Office made that decision prior to my arrival and there was nothing that I could do about it. The Lord was ordering my steps. My roommate modeled well living the Christian life. She read her Bible, prayed each morning and attended her Sabbath Teachings each week. She would often find a way to talk about her faith in my hearing and although I never joined her in her church attendance, I began to spend more than an occasional time reading the scriptures. I also observed and kept evaluating her actions. I was checking to see if she had been both a hearer and doer of the word that I read about in James 1:22. She maintained her steadfast walk and witness before me. It seemed she understood the words that Paul wrote to the Church at Corinth, when he said:

"You yourselves are our letter of recommendation (our credentials), written in your hearts, to be known (perceived, recognized) and read by everybody."
2 Cor.3:2 (AMP)

When I completed college, we went our separate ways and I continued to further my studies in the United States of America. It was here on 12/31/1972, that I gave my heart to Christ. What a change it has been as I have continued on to know Him.

A short time after, I realized how God drew me through the ministry of others – the Anglican priests, Father Persico and my college roommate. One planted another watered but He gave the increase.

I remembered Father Persico, and in a return visit to the Caribbean, inquired of him. How I just wanted to perhaps visit him, to give him my apology, and seek his forgiveness for my behavior years before. He had gone home to glory; but the memory of his words has lived with me throughout all these years.

A Prayer of Thanksgiving and Commission for Personal Ministry

Father, how I thank you for your loving kindness and tender mercies towards me; when I was rebellious you did not give up on me. You placed caring persons in my life that prayed and modeled the Christian life before me. Thank you for saving me. Lord, I know that there are many others who are faced with similar situations as I have so I ask for your grace and tender love to be continually extended to draw them to you. Send the right people into their lives and the right time to minister your love, truth and salvation. Bless the workers, whom you will choose as models that they may be consistent in representing you to the needy, and save those who have not known you as Savior and Lord. In Jesus' name I pray. Amen.

Chapter 1

Understanding God's Voice and Ways in Ministry

Show me your ways, O Lord; teach me your paths. Guide me in your truth and faithfulness and teach me. For You are the God of my salvation; for You [You only and altogether] do I wait [expectantly] all the day long. Ps. 25:4, 5 (AMP)

My salvation experience was accompanied with a shift in many friendships as I identified with the followers of Christ and the new walk of faith with Him. I had a new zeal for life. He gave me a hunger and thirst for biblical truths in His word, for knowledge and the pursuit of understanding of His nature. I desired to serve Him in whatever way possible. The word was becoming my spiritual food, instructions for life and service for Him in the Kingdom. I loved it, and thirsted for more and more of Him.

My first steps included membership in a Pentecostal church where I began to receive mid-weekly and Sunday teachings from the Pastor's sermons and bible study sessions. They focused on holy Christian living, doctrinal precepts of the church, and preparation for a loving, dutiful service to God in witnessing the saving grace of the Lord to non-Christians and inviting them to come to Christ.

I was eager to learn as much as possible and became involved with a group of ladies who were members in good standing in the church. I joined them in fellowship as they rotated meetings in their homes. For me it was a type of spiritual mentoring. They prayed for each other as well as for important issues of the day. Various aspects of the Word were often discussed and spiritual gifts manifested.

The fellowship had its merits and demerits. On the one hand there was *koinonia* or fellowship with each other which was a good thing. On the other hand, it was very controlling. I conformed to many of their traditions and norms.

Although, I received encouragement, and was growing in love, sharing and caring for others in the group, my relationship with God was underdeveloped. I took shelter in the group's knowledge of God and became co-dependent on the members. Whatever they said the Lord wanted us to do in prayer or in prophecy, I did. In that type of mentoring relationship, my personal focus on God was impaired. I was not personally hearing the voice of God. Each meeting I would wait to receive what God had to say from any one of at least three persons in the group.

Two experiences that urged me to Seek God's Voice for Your Self

(a) Less than a year after becoming a Christian, there was a youth convention in Birmingham, England. It happened during the time when I belonged to the special Christian women's group of which I have previously mentioned.

My daughter, then two years of age and I were attending the Convention as delegates. An arrangement was made for us to travel to Baltimore, to link up with the other delegates in that city on a set day. All the group members knew we were planning to attend the conference and I was excited.

Two days prior to our departure, one of the members whom I will call Darlene called me and strongly suggested I change my flight and leave a day earlier than scheduled. She said that it was to avoid problems that we would encounter if we traveled according to our original schedule. I became worried and fearful.

In obedience, to Darlene's council I changed my schedule to comply with what I thought was a prophecy and the voice of God. After all, she had prophesied to the group and her words were accepted. I was too naïve to know the difference.

Sometime later that day, I spoke with another group member and I related what I had done. She immediately upbraided me for changing the flight. "That message is not from God". She said. "God does not work like that and you should not have changed your flight." She continued. I was really feeling troubled. However, I continued with the new travel plan and left one day earlier as Darlene had recommended.

Arriving in Baltimore a day early, we had no accommodations for the night. The Church was not meeting that evening but rather the following day. No one expected us everywhere was closed. It was my first visit there. I felt lost and deceived by a false prophecy. God was merciful! He looked beyond my ignorance and naiveté and saw my need. He sent a total stranger to help us. This person introduced us to a family that lived close to the church and we were allowed to stay there for the night. Our very gracious hostess blessed us with some breakfast the following morning. God used those two persons in the ministry of helps and hospitality to get us through that ordeal.

When the day's preparations were put into place, the delegates all assembled and we joined them for the rest of the trip in accordance with the information we had originally received. The rest of the trip and experience overseas continued successfully.

(b) My second negative experience occurred during a visit to a Christian convention in Baltimore. Prior to the trip, Darlene counseled and convinced me to get rid of all apparel that made me appear worldly; that included the type of shoes I wore – specifically those that exposed both my heels and toes. I was so happy to be saved and to be a part of the family of believers, that I blindly accepted her advice for she presented herself as the mature Christian. In obedience, I got rid of most of my clothes and all those shoes that exposed my heels and toes. However, I soon found they were the ones that provided me the most comfort given the size and shape of my feet.

I was the driver for the entire eight hour trip to Baltimore. Upon our arrival, both of my feet were swollen and would not fit into my shoes. So, in order for me to participate in the worship and convention activities, I had to purchase a pair of sandals that exposed my heels and toes. Sandals at the time were the only thing that gave comfort to my feet.

There are some things that we learn by personal experience and others that we acquire through the testimony of other individuals. As a result of that incident, the Holy Spirit taught me that my salvation did not rest in my outer appearance, but rather in the inward condition of my heart that was surrendered to Him. At that point the following scripture became real to me.

"Rend your heart and not your garments, and turn unto the Lord your God". Joel 2:13a (AMP).

Subsequent to that experience, I repented to God for allowing others to control and manipulate me. I fasted and prayed for Him to deliver me from unhealthy soul ties, and asked Him to be the Master Teacher in my life.

The spiritual mentor's or minister's function is to help the mentored to know God personally, to train individuals to develop a listening ear to God and to increase faith in God among other things. Sometimes young Christians develop spiritual anemia and stagnant growth because of dominant, controlling spirits of some believers who are older in the faith. God is our loving heavenly Father who wants His children to know Him personally, to hear His voice, to commune with Him and obey Him through Jesus and His word. Jesus says:

"The sheep that are my own hear and are listening to My voice; And I know them, and they follow me". Jn. 10:27 (AMP).

God has a plan and purpose for every believer's life and He has clearly revealed it in this statement:

"For I know the thoughts and plans that I have for you, says the Lord. Thoughts and plans for welfare and peace and not for evil. To give you hope in your final outcome." Jer. 29:11 (AMP).

God also uses various means of bringing the believer into the wonderful experience of knowing Him. Sometimes it is through reading, studying, meditating on Him, through sermons, testimonies, and counseling; but always, it is as the result of prayer and obedience to His word.

As an individual takes God at His Word, that is, believing, meditating, receiving, and activating each precept by faith, God manifests the power, application and reality of that Word and of Himself. He guides you, and impresses in you specific steps as needed. The resulting experiences bring that person into an understanding of God, His voice, Word and ways. The greater the understanding, the closer the relationship with God becomes.

We need to be careful not to allow anything or anyone to usurp this Lordship of Christ in our lives. Here is a picture of the mentoring relationship between Eli and Samuel. Notice how Eli encouraged Samuel to listen and respond to God's voice.

> *"At that time Eli, whose eyesight had dimmed, so that he could not see, was lying down, in his own place. The lamp of God had not yet gone out of the temple of the Lord, where the ark of God was, and Samuel was lying down when the Lord called, Samuel! And he answered, Here am I. He ran unto Eli, and said. Here am I: for you called me. Eli said. I did not call you; lie down again. So he went and lay down. And the Lord called him again, Samuel! And Samuel arose and went to Eli, and said. Here am I: You did call me. Eli answered, I did not call you, my son: Lie down again. Now Samuel did not yet know the Lord, and the word of the Lord was not yet revealed unto him. And the Lord called Samuel the third time. And he went to Eli and said, Here am I; for you did call me. Then Eli perceived that the Lord was calling the boy. So Eli said unto Samuel, Go, and lie down: And if he calls you, you shall say, Speak, Lord; for thy servant is listening. So Samuel went and lay down in his place. And the Lord came and stood and called as at other times, Samuel! Samuel! Then Samuel answered, Speak, Lord, for your servant is listening."* 1 Sam. 3:2-10 (AMP)

It is so imperative to learn to recognize the voice of God early in one's Christian walk. As the Holy Spirit ministers to us, protects and nurtures our growth, we will be more apt to respond to Him, to be dependant on Him and less likely to follow wrong counsel from other sources including some Christians.

As a result of my experiences with Darlene, I desired to be alone with God, to spend more time in his word and to pray alone to God. I had a thirst and holy fear for Him. The Lord began to deal with me in my dreams and through images and transparencies that would flash before my closed eyes in twilight sleep.

When I Heard God's Voice for Myself

One morning very early before day break, I heard my name being called in the melody of a song with instructions for a plan of action that the Lord wanted me to pursue at work that day. Hallelujah! The Lord audibly ministered to me through His angel! I was ecstatic. He made me know that His voice was real and that I too could hear Him! He wanted to talk to me, as His child, and the sheep of His pasture.

> *"The sheep hear His voice, and He calls his own sheep by name and leads them out…..He goes before them; and the sheep follow Him, for they know His voice."* Jn.10:3b, 4 (NKJV)

I was amazed and joyfully wept. I obeyed the instructions that I received. The outcome was truly great! It established me on a pathway for future blessings that I needed in my job situation.

> *"O the depths of the riches both of wisdom and knowledge of God! How unsearchable are his judgments, and his ways past finding out!"*
> Rom. 11:33 (NKJV).

The experience drew me closer to God in daily devotions and personal bible study. I soon formulated some principles from His word that I wanted to live by, such as:

- My sufficiency is in Him.
- Neither anyone nor anything is to usurp His place in my life.
- The Holy Spirit within me is my Divine instructor and enabler to lead me in the green pastures of life.
- I must trust in Him with all my heart; and not lean unto my own understanding, but, in all my ways, acknowledge Him, and He will direct my path.

The Lord continued to encourage me as I delved deeper into His word. Some passages seemed as if they were highlighted in my spirit for special focus. Here are three such passages:

> *"The thief comes only in order to steal and kill and destroy.*
> *I came that they [referring to believers] may have and enjoy life, and have it in abundance (to the full, till it overflows). I am the Good Shepherd. The Good Shepherd risks and lays down His (own) for the sheep."*
> Jn.10:10, 11 (AMP) paraphrased for emphasis.

> *"Those who trust in, lean on, and confidently hope in the Lord are like Mount Zion, which cannot be moved but abides and stands fast forever. As the mountains are round about Jerusalem, so the Lord*

is round about His people from this time forth and forever. For the scepter of wickedness shall not rest upon the land of the (uncompromisingly) righteous, lest the righteous (God's People), stretch forth their hand to iniquity and apostasy. Ps.125:1, 3 (AMP).

"The Angel of the Lord encamps around those who fear Him (who revere and worship Him with awe) and each of them He delivers. Oh, taste and see that the Lord (our God) is good! Blessed (happy, fortunate, to be envied) is the man who trusts and takes refuge in Him!" Ps.34:7, 8 (AMP)

When God Ministered Healing Through Me

One weekend while still being a very young Christian, a very unusual thing happened at my home. My sister was visiting from Montreal and became ill. She was unable to urinate and needed urgent attention. She had no insurance making going to the hospital for emergency center a last resort.

I called my pastor seeking a prayer for healing for my sister. I was in compliance with the traditional teaching I received in that Church. We were not ordained elders and were to observe the writing of James 5:14, 15 that states:

"Is anyone among you sick? Let him call the elders of the church; and let them pray over him, anointing him with oil in the name of the Lord. And the prayer of faith will save the sick, and the Lord will raise him up; and if he has committed sins, he will be forgiven." James 5:14, 15 (NKJV).

It so happened that the Pastor was unavailable, and neither could I reach the other ordained elders of the church. We were faced with a serious situation, what could I do?

I began to pray and the Holy Spirit directed me to take some oil that was in my home, to pray over it and anoint my sister with it in the Name of Jesus. At His instruction, I then laid my hands on her stomach and prayed for her healing. It was my first experience doing something of that nature. Miraculously the Lord moved – healing and delivering my sister. I was amazed and at the same time very much relieved. My sister was well again! Hallelujah!

Through that experience the Lord taught me that:

- He is the Lord God Almighty, strong to deliver and to save.
- He is my instant help in the time of trouble.
- He is the God of miracles, releasing His supernatural power through whomsoever He wills. Gender and titles were not issues for Him.

What a way to learn? What God wanted was faith in Him and obedience to Him. I was to respect and honor the leadership in the church, but to know Him for myself and be willing to serve others under His direction. Isn't it awesome to know that the word of God records

> *"There is [now no distinction] neither Jew nor Greek, there is neither slave nor free, there is not male and female: for you are all one in Christ Jesus"?*
> Gal.3:28 (AMP)

God is seeking for men and women everywhere, who love Him and understand that we are His workmanship created in Him for His good pleasure and manifestation of His glory in the earth. We are His agents for good, meeting the needs of whomsoever He puts in our path. He is depending on us to rightly discern his voice – whether directly or through others in prophesy. Let us be courageous, unafraid, and unashamed. Let us allow Him to use us for His kingdom and glory. God will show He is strong on behalf of all whose hearts are perfect towards Him and who seek Him out in relationship. As we abide in Him, and He in us, whatever we ask for in His will and in the name of Jesus, shall be done for us. What a blessed assurance.

A Prayer to Hear God's Voice and Understand His Ways

Heavenly Father, I thank you for being our shield, teacher and protector. Thank you for the experiences that we go through knowing that you will cause them to work for our good, as we mature in you. Be gracious to those who have been led astray, have been disillusioned or deceived by the work of the enemy. Please forgive, heal, restore and strengthen their hold on you. Help us all to know your voice as we meditate on your word and give you worship. Sensitize us when you speak and grant us an understanding of how you operate in us and around us. Lead us continually in your word and draw us ever closer to you. In Jesus' name I pray. Amen.

Chapter 2

Understanding the Concept of Ministry

"Laboring together [as God's fellow workers] with Him then, we beg of you not to receive the grace of God in vain [that merciful kindness by which God exerts His holy influence on souls and turns them to Christ, keeping and strengthening them]—Do not receive it to no purpose." 2Cor. 6:1, 2 (AMP)

When God created the world, He fashioned us in His image and likeness. We are to lean on Him in all things, to relate to each other as a community of believers, and to serve one another in love. You may be a king, an astronaut, a judge, or ruler; you may be a parent, doctor, an executive, a teacher, housewife, electrician, or servant. No one is an island unto himself. We are inter-related. God depends on us and we depend on Him and others like ourselves to minister His love, truth and power in the earth.

We possess physical, emotional and spiritual needs, and even the greatest psychologist cannot satisfy the spiritual needs of the soul. The job alone won't do it. It may provide prestige, honor, power, even financial prosperity and a sense of security, but there are often burdens of the heart and emotional longings of the soul that need healing and wholeness. This fulfillment comes through the personal work of the Holy Spirit and the involvement of others in ministry. God wants us to have an equal measure of spiritual, emotional and physical prosperity. It is a part of His purpose for all believers. Here is what His word says:

> *"Beloved, I pray that you may prosper in every way and [that your body] may keep well, even as [I know] your soul keeps well and prospers."* 3 Jn 2 (AMP).

The word ministry is a noun (in Hebrew *diakonia*) derived from the phrase *eis diakonian* which translated means to minister, to do service. Therefore, anyone who renders a service unto the Lord can be a termed a minister. The process of ministry divinely releases the relevant attributes of God into the lives of the recipients. God's love, mercy, grace, hope, peace, power, might and understanding, His justice, righteousness and truth, are all imparted through faith in Him. Ministers serve by activating or facilitating this faith. God wants to reveal Himself to the ignorant; to bring forgiveness, healing and deliverance from all types of oppression; and Salvation to the lost. Let us examine how ministry was first done in the Old Testament time and its development in the New Testament Church.

Old Testament Ministry – Mediation and Guidance

Ministry was administered mainly through the office of the priest - notably Aaron, his descendants, the Levites and the prophets.

> *"From among the Israelites take your brother Aaron and his sons with him, that he may minister*

to Me in the priest's office, even Aaron, Nadab, and Abihu, Eleazar and Ithamar, Aaron's sons...The holy garments of Aaron shall pass to his descendants who succeed him, to be anointed in them and to be consecrated and ordained in them. And that son who is [high] priest in his stead shall put them on [each day for] seven days, when he comes into the Tent of the Meeting to minister in the holy place."
Exod. 28:1; 29:29, 30 (AMP)

"And the Lord said to Moses,.....Take the Levites from among the children of Israel, and cleanse them...You shall present the Levites before the Tent of Meeting, and assemble the whole congregation. And you shall present the Levites before the Lord, and the Israelites shall put their hands upon the Levites, and Aaron shall offer the Levites before the Lord as a wave offering from the Israelites, and on their behalf, that they may do the service of the Lord......For they are wholly given unto me from among the Israelites; instead of all who open every womb, the firstborn of all the of Israelites, I have taken the Levites for Myself." Num.8:1, 6, 9 -11, 16 (AMP).

The ministry of the prophets was done through men and women who first had a personal, momentous encounter with God. Isaiah had a vision, Jeremiah heard God's voice, and Moses had the burning bush experience. These individuals both proclaimed God's council to man and served in drawing and presenting people to God. Take for example Moses, as a friend of God, who prayed and challenged the mixed multitude coming out of Egypt, to purity, holiness and the worship of Jehovah. He counseled and agonized in intercession before God for the children of Israel several times as they journeyed from Egypt through the wilderness to the outskirts of

Canaan. Here are two examples of Moses leading the crowd of over three million, murmuring, rebellious people out of Egypt. See how he ministered to their needs.

Having left Egypt, they arrived at Marah, where they ran out of pure water to drink. The waters at Marah were bitter and the children of Israel murmured against Moses, saying,

> *"What shall we drink? And he cried unto the Lord; and the Lord showed him a tree, which he cast into the waters, the waters were made sweet. There [the Lord] made for them a statute and an ordinance, and there He proved them."* Exod.15:24, 25 (AMP).

Later they reached the base of Mount Sinai. Moses went up into the mountain to converse with God, and was delayed in his return. Aaron, the second in command led the crowd into preparing a golden calf for idol worship, reminiscent of their Egyptian lifestyle. When God saw that, He said to Moses:

> *"Go down, because your people, whom you brought up out Egypt, have become corrupt. They have been quick to turn away from what I commanded them and have made themselves an idol, cast in the shape of a calf. They have bowed down to it, and sacrificed to it and have said,*
> *'These are your gods, O Israel, who brought you out of Egypt'. "I have seen these people," the Lord said to Moses, "And they are a stiff-necked people. Now leave me alone so that my anger may burn against them and that I may destroy them. Then will I make you a great nation." But Moses sought the favor of the Lord his God. "O Lord," he said, "why should your anger burn against your people whom you brought out of Egypt with your great power and mighty hand? Why should the Egyptians say, 'it was*

with evil intent that He brought them out to kill them in the mountains and wipe them off the face of the earth'? Turn from your fierce anger; relent and do not bring disaster on your people. Remember your servants Abraham, Isaac and Israel, to whom you swore by your own self: 'I will make your descendants as numerous as the stars in the sky and I will give your descendants all this land I promised them, and it will be their inheritance forever.'" Then the Lord relented and did not bring on his people the disaster he had threatened. Ex. 32:7-14 (NIV)

Then as Moses approached the reveling idolatrous crowd at the foot of the mountain, he became so angry that he destroyed the tablets with the commandments that God had given to him. He made Aaron and the crowd destroy the calf; acknowledge their sin and then he purified the camp. The following day, he went before the Lord and besought God's mercy and forgiveness for the sins of the multitude. He said:

"Oh, what a great sin these people have committed! They have made themselves gods of gold. But now, please forgive their sin— But if not, then blot me out of your book, you have written. The Lord replied to Moses, whoever has sinned has sinned against me I will blot out of the book. Now go, lead the people to the place I spoke of and my angel will go before you. However, when the time comes for me to punish, I will punish them for their sins." Exod. 32:31-34 (NIV)

Ministry requires compassion, advocacy, love and commitment as we bring God to our fellowmen and present them to God.

New Testament Church Ministry - Peer Support & Ordained Instruction

In the New Testament Church birthed on the day of Pentecost, the term 'ministry' expanded to include more than designated office leaders i.e., apostles, overseers, bishops, pastors, evangelists and teachers. The five-fold ministry was established for equipping the body of Christ to serve God and one another. Paul defines it well in his letter to the Church at Ephesus in this statement:

> *"And He Himself gave some to be apostles; some prophets, some evangelists, and some, pastors and teachers, for the equipping of the saints for the work of the ministry, for the edifying of the body of Christ. Till we all come to the unity of the faith and the knowledge of the Son of God, to the measure of the stature of the fullness of Christ."* Eph. 4:11, 12 (NKJV)

Those who accepted Christ as Savior and continued in the knowledge of Him, were to be involved in ministry after being taught or trained by the apostles, prophets, evangelists, pastors and teachers. They were also to be endowed with power by the Holy Spirit. As it was then, so it is to be encouraged and developed in the Churches today. This enables ordinary people to do great exploits for God without fear. Let us look at some examples of kingdom citizens at work in the New Testament era that is relevant for us today.

Priscilla and Aquila

Priscilla and Aquila, were a husband and wife team, we read about in the book of Acts of the Apostles, 18:24-26. This saved couple had great insight and spiritual understanding of the scriptures. They actually held a church in their home and the Lord allowed them to minister, and to serve several believers including Paul, the Apostle who stayed at their home for eighteen months. Paul gratefully acknowledged their service to him in a portion of his letter to the Church from Rome. He writes:

> *"Greet Priscilla and Aquila my fellow workers in Christ Jesus, who risked their own necks for my life, to whom not only I give thanks, but also all the churches of the Gentiles. Likewise greet the church that is in their house."* Rom.16: 3, 4 (NKJV).

Priscilla and Aquila were also instrumental in enriching the ministry of Apollos. Apollos was an educated Alexandrian Jew, and an orator whose knowledge of the scriptures was limited to the Baptism of John. He needed a breadth of understanding of God's word. The couple seized the opportunity to do so for God's glory.

> *"So he (Apollos) began to speak boldly in the synagogue:*
> When Aquila and Priscilla had heard him, they took him aside, and expounded unto him the way of God more accurately." Acts 18:26 (NKJV).

Lydia

Lydia showed a generous compassion and hospitality to God's servant Paul. She was a merchant woman, who loved to pray and was described as *"a worshipper of God"* according to Acts 16:14. She was a Gentile from Thyatira, who became converted under Paul's ministry on his second missionary journey. She was so excited about Paul and Silas, that immediately after the other members of her household accepted salvation and were baptized, she invited and served both missionary servants of God into her home before they proceeded on their journey to Philippi. These were her words:

> *"If you consider me a believer in the Lord,"* she said, *"come and stay at my house"*. Acts 16:15 (NIV)

Of course, Paul and Silas accepted the offer and she ministered to their needs in her home.

Tychicus

Tychicus was a much-loved brother and faithful ministering assistant or deacon that Paul used to take information back to the church at Ephesus and to give an account of Paul's work at Colosse according to Colossians 4:7.

Epaphras

Paul named Epaphras, as a servant of Christ, a prayer intercessor, who labored fervently for the saints to *"Stand firm in all the will of God, mature and fully assured"*. Col. 4:12 (NIV).

Stephen

Stephen, who was one of the first martyrs of the early Church, was a deacon whom God used to spread the good news of the Gospel, and to do great wonders and miracles among the people in Asia according to Acts 6: 8 (NIV)

And Others

Peter's mother-in-law, after receiving a miracle of healing by a touch from Jesus, arose and waited on them Matt. 8:14 (NIV).

A woman of questionable character, at the Sychar Well in Samaria, went into the city witnessing and persuaded people to come and meet Jesus, after she had obtained personal salvation and deliverance from Him. Jn. 4:28 – 30 (NIV).

Mary ministered to Jesus by pouring about a pint of pure nard, an expensive perfume on Jesus' feet and wiping His feet with her hair, while at a dinner given to honor Jesus in Bethany. Jn. 12:3 (NIV)

Ministering Unto God - Worship

Believers are called to minister to God in worship, for He will minister to us." *He whose walk is blameless will minister to me."* says Psalms 101:6b (NIV). It is often during times of worship that we receive God's counsel for direction and ministry. Saul and Barnabas had that experience according to Acts 13:2. As the apostles worshipped the Lord in prayer and fasting, the Holy Spirit chose them for their missionary appointment.

The Bible gives several other examples of lay persons serving in ministry in the Kingdom of God. Their examples show us that we too can and should minister according to the needs of our fellowmen.

It's my hope dear reader that if are a Christian and you previously entertained any doubts about your ability to minister, that you will now endeavor to become a fellow worker with God. We are all ministers of God's abundant grace and are called to the ministry of reconciliation of souls to Him. The Holy Spirit has given His seal of approval on the body of believers, through the anointing which is the Divine enablement to achieve the things of God. Let us be bold and step out using what we know and doing what the Holy Spirit guides us to do.

In the early church, access to bibles and written materials was very limited, but the disciples did not depend solely on those avenues to reach to world. They all went about ministering with the power of God that resided in them. Peter and John ministered healing to a crippled man at the Beautiful Gate on their way to prayer. Jesus performed a miracle there before their very eyes by restoring healing to the beggar's previously paralyzed feet and ankles. Peter said:

> *"Silver and gold I do not have, but such as I have I give you. In the name of Jesus Christ on Nazareth, rise up and walk." Taking him by the right hand, he helped him up, and instantly the man's feet and ankle became strong. He jumped to his feet and began to walk."* Acts 3:6-8a (NIV)

We, as believers need to emulate the actions of the early disciples today. God wants the church to be totally delivered from inhibition and many traditions that crept into it following the era of Constantine in Rome, when persecution, imprisonment, fear and compromise attacked the body of Christ. Today, there are many religions that compete for the soul of man, spreading anti-Christ beliefs. Deception continues to spread over the whole world.

God is depending on the church who is the body of believers to declare the truth of His word; for Salvation is found only in Jesus Christ, the Son of the Living God. There is urgency, in light of His imminent return that you and I do this.

In this season before Jesus comes back for His church, many who are lost and outside the gate of safety in Christ will be won through our witness, the demonstration of miraculous healings, signs and wonders. We are to be living epistles read by all men. The supernatural power for signs wonders and miracles resides within believers and is awaiting release through obedience and dependence on the Holy Spirit. God wants to use us to see people set free not only on Sundays but everyday of the week: in the places of assembly for worship, in homes, the market place, prisons, hospitals, recreational facilities, buses, trains and other vehicles of transportation on sea, in the air and everywhere. St. Paul puts it this way:

> "For [even the whole] creation (all nature) waits expectantly and longs earnestly for God's sons to be made known [waits for the revealing, the disclosing of their sonship]. And not only the creation, but we ourselves too, who have enjoyed the first fruits of the [Holy] Spirit [a foretaste of the blissful things to come] Groan inwardly as we wait for the redemption of our bodies [from sensuality and the grave, which will reveal] our adoption (our manifestation as God's sons). Rom. 8:19, 23 (AMP)

This is our challenge believers. It's a divine mandate, and may God open our understanding and give us the courage to do His will. Ministry is really whatever one does for the kingdom that glorifies God. We need to say 'Yes' to God from now on, and trust Him to work out the details through our experiences. Personally, I find that ministry is bearing fruit. The support is the Holy Spirit. Let us simply allow the Holy Spirit to order our steps as He controls our lives that we may produce fruit that is pleasing to God.

A Prayer of Submission

Father you have shown us through examples from your word that the concept of ministry fulfils many and varied undertakings for your kingdom. We realize it is a work of your Holy Spirit in our vessels, and that there are many needs for which you patiently await our commitment to serve you. We present ourselves to you today. Remove all ignorance and hindrances we pray. Grant us the courage to be faithful, to lean on you and to do all things to bring glory to your name. I ask in Jesus' name. Amen.

Chapter 3

Called and Chosen for Ministry

"Also I heard the voice of the Lord, saying, whom shall I send? And who will go for us? Then said I, Here am I; send me." Is. 6:8 (AMP)

The prophet Isaiah lived in the eighth century BC. He was mightily used by God to deliver prophetic messages of God's pending judgment on the Southern Kingdom of Judah, unless they repented of their sins. It is interesting to note how God prepares someone for His work. In Isaiah's case God allowed him to have a mentor, King Uzziah, in the earlier stages of his life. The mentor was not perfect, no one is, but when God was ready to prepare Isaiah for his life's work in ministry, He permanently removed the king from Isaiah's life. Oftentimes, individuals are brought into our lives, but only for a season as a part of God's plan. The disconsolate Isaiah sought comfort in worship to God. It was there, that the spiritual blindness was removed from his eyes enabling him for greatness in ministry as he beheld an awesome vision of the holiness of God.

"In the year the King Uzziah died, [in a vision] I saw the Lord sitting upon a throne, high and lifted up, and

> *the skirts of His train filled the [most holy part of the] temple. Above Him stood the seraphim; each had six wings: with two [each] covered his [own] face, and with two [each] covered his feet, and with two [each] flew. And one cried to another and said, Holy, holy, holy is the Lord of hosts; the whole earth is full of His glory! And the foundations of the thresholds shook at the voice of him who cried, and the house was filled with smoke. Then said I, Woe is me! For I am undone and ruined, because I am a man of unclean lips and I dwell in the midst of people with unclean lips; for my eyes have seen the King the Lord of hosts! Then flew one of the seraphim [heavenly beings] to me, having a live coal in his hand......He touched my mouth and said, behold this has touched your lips your iniquity and guilt are taken away and your sin is completely atoned for and forgiven. Also I heard the voice of the Lord, saying, whom shall I send? And who will go for us? Then said I, here am I; send me.*
> Isaiah 6: 1-8 (AMP)

The experience brought a total transformation in Isaiah. He surrendered his impoverished spiritual and emotional state to God. God healed him and then spoke to him, commissioning him for his lifetime work with the leaders and people of Southern Judah. Isaiah willingly accepted God's call to ministry.

There are other incidents in the Bible that illustrate how God called men and women to serve Him. For example Samuel was a young priest assistant to Eli, who heard his name being called three times while he rested one night. His call did not come with a vision like Isaiah. The story is found in the I Samuel 3:1-10.

Samuel was called as a child. He did not even know much about the word. He was a trainee performing the daily physical duties of the temple. Sometimes when God calls, it may not be very clear to the untrained ear. When that person is doubtful, God has a way of making Himself known to him or her. Has He been calling you?

Moses was forty years old when he recognized God's calling on his life. He experienced a supernatural visitation and the voice of The Angel of God communing with him.

"And the angel of Lord appeared to him in flames of fire from within a bush. Moses saw that though the bush was on fire it did not burn up. So Moses thought." I will go over and see this strange sight— why the bush does not burn up". When the Lord saw that he had gone over to look,
God called to him from the within the bush," Moses, Moses!" and Moses said, "Here I am."
Exod. 3:2-4 (NIV).

Paul saw a light from heaven flash around him as he traveled on a Damascus road. He fell to the ground and heard a voice saying:

"Saul, Saul. Why are you persecuting me?"
Acts 9:3 (AMP).

It was then that Paul recognized that the voice was Jesus. There was a brief dialogue after which Paul experienced three days of blindness and humbling before the Savior. He accepted the commission to bear the tidings of the Gospel to the Gentiles and kings and the descendants of Israel, for the rest of life. You can read this in Acts 9:8.

In my personal experience, I saw a light like a star and heard the Lord's voice speak within me. He said:

> *"I am this dark world's light, look unto me, the morn shall rise, and all your days, be bright."*

It was then that I totally surrendered my life to Jesus and have endeavored to seek and serve Him ever since.

Have you accepted your call to serve Him? If not, it is not too late to accept to His wooing.

Let us be ever mindful that born-again believers are called to 'the ministry of reconciliation'.

> *"But all things are from God, who through Jesus Christ reconciled us to Himself [received us into favor, brought us into harmony with Himself] and gave us the ministry of reconciliation [that by word and deed we might aim to bring others into harmony with Him]."* 2 Cor.5:18 (AMP)

Salvation brings transformation through the renewal of the mind from the old carnal nature to birth a new zeal and desire to know God. It requires spending time with Him in prayer, reading, meditation and activating those principles you've learned in the Word as you go along. The call of God involves repentance, and forgiveness of others who hurt you. It is laying aside all the weights and the sins that so easily beset you and drag you down. Preparation begins with getting to know Jesus personally in the Word. Paul puts it this way:

> *"Therefore then, since we are surrounded by so great a cloud of witnesses [who have borne testimony of the Truth], let us strip off and throw away every encumbrance (unnecessary weights) and that sin which so readily (deftly and cleverly) clings and entangles us, and let us run with patient endurance and steady active persistence the appointed course*

of the race that is set before us. Looking away [from all that will distract] to Jesus who is the Leader and Source of our faith [giving the first incentive for our belief] and is also its Finisher [bringing into maturity and perfection]." Heb. 12:1,2a (AMP)

Responding to the call also entails a commitment in the pursuit of true holiness, living by faith in God and standing on the promises in His word. You will need to be a part of a strong Bible-believing church where you can be taught the rudiments of His word including, how to listen, recognize and obey the voice of God.

"My sheep hear my voice, and I know them, and they know me." Jn 10:27 9 (NKJV).

God loves to speak through His Word that is Spirit, life, counsel, knowledge, wisdom, guidance, instruction in righteousness and is the voice of God. Sometimes He impresses His will in one's spirit in a still inaudible way.

There are other times when God uses pastoral messages coming from the pulpit, or a word of knowledge or prophecy, that is the manifestation of one of the gifts. Some individuals testify of receiving vivid dreams, visions and supernatural angelic visitation. The most important thing is to be trained to know and obey the voice and Spirit of God.

Consistent growth involves persistent asking, seeking and knocking at the doors of scripture, observing teachings on the word provided by the anointed church leadership, participating in ministry opportunities and receiving the testimonies of over comers. Testimonies that glorify God are important. They show forth God's mighty power, style and results, as well as stir the listener's faith to expect great things from God when he or she takes heed to and obeys the word.

A further necessity for growth is that you habitually consecrate your mind and will to God through fasting, praying and spending time in His Presence. Strive to allow nothing to crowd out your planned special times with God. Worship Him, sing love songs to Him and ponder on the lyrics as you sing to Him. The Lord will respond to your seeking and give you the desires of your heart. David experienced this and wrote it in the Psalms.

"Delight thyself also in the Lord, and He will give you the desires and secret petitions of your heart.
Ps. 37: 4 (AMP).

It is absolutely God's will for believers to know His voice and heed His council so let us have expectation and obey the voice of God.

Chosen for Ministry

Believers in ministry are elected by God according to the foreknowledge of God, from the foundation of the world, through the drawing power of His Spirit, and acceptance of the finished work of Jesus Christ at the Cross. This is a blessed privilege for there are many who are called but only a few are chosen.

Chosen believers enter into a covenant relationship with God to obey Him, to worship Him, to serve and to honor Him through "fruit bearing", i.e. ministry. God in turn makes available to us, all the promises in His Word, on the condition that we are willing and obedient to Him. We inherit the blessings of Salvation and He grants us whatsoever we desire and ask in His will and in Jesus' Name. What a promise! As we keep our covenant of devotion and submission to Him, God gives us wisdom, understanding, knowledge and revelation so that we may do His will through the power of Holy Spirit resident in us. Paul reminds us that

> *"We have this treasure in earthen vessels that the excellence of the power may be of God and not of us."* 2 Cor. 4:7 (NKJV)

Chosen people are special and very important to God. He keeps us as the apple of His eye. Hallelujah! We are precious to Him. We are His jewels in the kingdom and a holy nation. Peter clearly expresses this in his writing for he says:

> *"But you are a chosen race, a royal priesthood, and dedicated nation, [God's] own purchased, special people, that you may set forth the wonderful deeds and display the virtues and perfections of him who called you out of darkness into his marvelous light.*
> 1 Pet 2: 9 (AMP)

God has a plan in every circumstance we face in life. Nothing is without His knowledge and scrutiny, even the tough days. The psalmist David says

> *"The steps of a [good] man are directed and established by the Lord when He delights in his way [and He busies himself with his every step].*
> Ps. 37:23 (AMP)

Therefore, when you and I accept who we are in Christ that is, being called and chosen of Him, let us consider maintaining our focus on Him no matter what circumstances that life throws at us, for God will work out every situation for our good. Trials are tests of our faith and commitment to endure to the end. Trials aim at bringing us into maturity and total dependence on God as He molds and fashions us into the image of His Son.

> *"Dear friends, do not be surprised at the painful trial you are suffering, as though something strange were happening to you. But rejoice that you participate in the sufferings of Christ, so that you may be overjoyed when His glory is revealed.* 1 Pet 4:12,13 (NIV)

Every victory is to be a blessing both to you and to someone else's life. This happens as we testify of the greatness of God in our circumstances. Each time we do this, we are giving God the chance to deliver someone else that is having a similar situation. The testimony of our experiences serves to build faith in the hearers. It encourages believers to have greater expectations of God, who has no respect of persons. What He does for one, He will do for all who believe in Him.

Christ is loving, kind, meek, gentle, merciful, longsuffering, peaceful, faithful and full of joy. He is not fickle, nor pretentious, and there is no hypocrisy in Him. He is not boastful. He is genuine, righteous and forgiving. He is all wisdom, knowledge, goodness, justice, holiness, power and truth. He is a winner, and never loses a battle.

In order to bear similar life-fruit, we must abide in Jesus, yield to Him and draw from Him. How we react and conduct ourselves in situations determine the nature of fruit we bear. A natural tree does not produce fruit until it is mature. So a believer needs to mature in Christ before that person can bear fruit. Fruit bearing is the outcome of the right attitude, obedience and the manifestation of the nature of Christ in interactions with others whether they are saved or unsaved. We are Christ's imitators, and must endeavor to always do the things that please Jesus.

Some believers hold back in ministering to others in the kingdom because of their feeling of insecurity and inadequacy. Do not allow such feelings to hinder you, for it is Christ in you who does the work. You and I are mere vessels for His honor and glory. He uses our bodies, shapes, sizes, personalities, color, temperaments, ambition, passion, testimonies and experiences to transform the lives of others for His glory. Freely we receive of God's grace, freely we aught to introduce Him to others.

A Prayer of the Call and Chosen

Lord, thank you for calling and choosing us your mouthpiece, hands and feet in the Kingdom. Thank you for your plan for us to bear fruit for your kingdom. We recognize that there is much that we do not know nor understand and sometimes in times of trials, we buckle and may fail you in ignorance. We repent of past errors and ask for your forgiveness. Pour out your special grace and anointing upon us and please bless us to know and follow your word as well as spiritual leading now and in the future. I pray in the name of Jesus, Amen.

Chapter 5

Responding to the Call of Ministry

Not by might, nor by power, but by my Spirit, says the Lord of hosts." Zech. 4:6 (NKJV)

The Bible tells of a time in Israel's history, when after the death of Joshua, God raised up a number of judges to lead the nation of the Jews in the land of Canaan. The Canaanites were not totally destroyed during Joshua's lifetime. For that reason, each tribe was left to complete God's mandate to Joshua, which was, to utterly destroy the Canaanites that dwelt in Jericho. God never wanted the pagan influences of the Canaanites to corrupt the Israelites. So far, the plan had failed:

> "Manasseh did not drive out the inhabitants of Beth Sheam...When Israel was strong; they put the Canaanites under tribute...... Nor did Napthali...... but dwelt among the Canaanites... The Amorites forced the children of Dan into the mountains."
> Jud. 1:27-34 (NKJV).

The children of Israel were disobedient to God and so none of them succeeded against the stubborn, determined Canaanites. One day the angel of God went up from Gilgal to Bokim and spoke to the Israelites saying:

> *"I led you up from Egypt and brought you to the land which I swore to your fathers; and said 'I will never break a covenant with you. And you shall make no covenant with the inhabitants of this land; you shall tear down their altars'. But you have not obeyed my voice. Why have you done this? Therefore, I also will not drive them out before you; but they shall be thorns in your side, and their gods shall be a snare to you."* Jud. 2:1-4 (NKJV)

Many of the Israelites inter-married the pagans and worshipped pagan gods. When they faced hardships, for turning their backs on God, some would cry unto the Lord for deliverance. The Lord then raised up someone, usually a judge, who would intercede on behalf of the nation and the people would experience deliverance for a season. The cycle was repeated continually. Against this background, the Midianites and the Amalekites oppressed the Israelites. The Israelites had to live in dens and caves in the mountains. Whenever they planted their crops, however, these nomadic intruders would invade at harvest time, with their camels and livestock and totally impoverish the Israelites' livelihood leaving nothing for their ox, sheep or donkeys. Many Israelites cried out unto God for deliverance.

One day the Angel of the Lord appeared unto Gideon as he threshed wheat in the winepress in order to conceal it from the Midianites. The Angel said: *"The Lord is with you, you mighty man of valor."* Jud. 6: 12 (NKJV).

A dialogue ensued during which time God asked Gideon to go and serve his people against their enemies. Gideon experienced a range of emotions. First of all, he became afraid for his life, for he knew that no one who had seen God could live. The Angel dealt with that issue. Then Gideon entertained worry and expressed his feelings of inadequacy and inferiority complex. He spoke of his heritage and meager family status.

"But Lord", Gideon asked: "How can I save Israel? My clan is the weakest in Manasseh, and I am the least in my family?"

The Lord answered:

*"I will be with you, and you will strike down **all** the Midianites together."* Jud. 6:15, 16 (NIV)

The story goes on to tell of how God strengthened Gideon, how He gave Gideon the strategy for warfare and gave victory to the Israelites, so that they continued to live in peace for the next forty years. You can read the entire story in the Book of Judges Chapters 6 and 7.

We can gain some insights from this account of how God prepared and used Gideon to serve Him in the deliverance of the Israelites. God can and does use ordinary people to fulfill His purposes in this world. Gideon was an ordinary citizen who was afraid, lacked courage and felt inadequate, insecure and perhaps socially unacceptable. Like Gideon, God also knows our lineage, ability, areas of insufficiency, where we live, our past and present experiences. He knows everything about us. After all, it is He who has made us. We are His workmanship created for good works. God calls us just as we are.

Are you holding back? Some of us say:

- We are not ready, there are some situations we want to fix first, or after we have completed a certain milestone in our career.
- We are too old or we don't know enough or even that we are too shy.

We need to surrender to God and lay all the excuses at the feet of Jesus. He can and will work out His plan in us.

The Bible records the works of many ordinary individuals through whom God manifested His power and glory. He will use you as well if you surrender your will and abilities to Him. Will you accept the challenge? Here are a few biblical examples:

Moses: Responding to Issues of Personal Past & Age

God used Moses, who was a murderer, to minister to Pharaoh and to demonstrate His plan for the deliverance of over three million oppressed Jews in Egypt. Moses complained of a speech impediment. He was over eighty years old when God called him to this mission. Don't allow our age to hinder us. There are many areas in which God can use a seasoned adult such as:

- Ministering to the sick and shut in. One can visit or use the telephone as the means of reaching out and meeting some needs of this special group.
- Seasoned adults can mentor younger believers in the faith. They can volunteer in Child Development Ministries;
- They can do telephone follow ups on New Converts;
- Some may even become involved in designing and making religious tracks as tools for witnessing.
- Seasoned adults can become pillars of support and intercessors on behalf of church, missionaries, civic

leaders and others on the firing line for the cause of Christ.

Age should not be a problem in ministry. God has called the young because of their strength and the old because of their wisdom. So, if you are not involved in ministry, it is time to start.

Rahab: Responding to Class Issues

God used Rahab, a prostitute, to minister to the spies whom Joshua had sent out to secretly check out the land of Canaan. Her social class did not hinder her ministry. She hid those spies in the attic of her residence and out-smarted her governmental authorities. It is possible that she was afraid and perhaps felt really vulnerable for she resided in Jericho; but, she was an intelligent woman, and had an insight into what God was going to do for the children of Israel. These were her words:

> *"I know that the Lord has given you the land, that the fear of you has fallen upon us and that all the inhabitants of the land are fainthearted because of you. For we have heard how the Lord dried up the water of the Red Sea for you when you came out of Egypt, and what you did to the two kings of the Amorites who were on the other side of the Jordan, Sihon and Og, whom you utterly destroyed. And as soon as we heard these things, our hearts melted; neither did there remain any more courage in anyone because of you, for the Lord your God, He is the God of heaven above and on earth."* Josh. 2: 9-11(NKJV)

It is amazing the wisdom of this woman. She accepted and confessed Yahweh to be the supreme God of heaven and

earth. This was different from the pagan gods of her culture. She took the risk by faith, entered into a covenant with the spies that God honored. That action allowed her to minister to the spies need for protection which eventually brought her salvation. Her faith and courage enabled her to become a link in the lineage of King David and Jesus Christ the King of Kings, for she became the mother of Boaz, in the ancestry of Joseph, Jesus' earthly father. Matt. 1:5, 16 (NKJV).
We never can tell where a decision for God will take us, or what a commitment to serve Him and others will do, but God honors right decisions and releases rewards in due time.

Naaman's Maid: Responding to Issues of Victimization & Alienation

Here is a story in which the Bible tells of a slave girl, who was captured and taken from her family, during a battle between Syria and Israel. Naaman was captain of the king's army that invaded Israel. He brought back the girl as a slave at the end of the battle. He placed her to serve his wife as a maid. During that time, Naaman developed the incurable disease of leprosy. The maid had faith in God. She knew the power of God had worked through the Prophet Elijah in the past. She over looked her circumstances being deprived of her real family life, and any other possible injustice that might have been done to her. She saw a need. Her master was gravely sick and needed a miracle of healing. She addressed her mistress and said:

> *"If only my master were with the prophet who is in Samaria! For he would heal him of his leprosy."*
> 2 Ki. 5:2 (NKJV).

Her words, faith and gentle persuasion eventually enabled leprous Naaman to receive his healing through the ministry of the prophet Elijah. Regardless of our circumstances in life, if we are willing, God can and wants to use those experiences to help others for His glory.

Have you ever been faced with situations and wondered why? We often get upset, even become vindictive; but if only we can get the strength to hold on, the Lord will give the grace and provide a way out of that situation. The maid's action made it possible for God to show how He transcends barriers of nationality, race, social and economic status, to meet human needs. Remember the girl was an Israelite and ironically the only hope for a cure for Naaman came through one of the very people against whom he fought. Isn't God a marvel?

Ministry in an Unlikely Circumstance

One day, a friend of mine gave me a testimony of how his puppy was very ill. He had several visits with the animal to the vet. Each visit he would witness of the goodness of God and what faith in God could do. The puppy seemed at first not to be improving. She was diagnosed with pneumonia.

The owner called members of our prayer group and requested prayer for the healing of the puppy. That was a new experience for some of us as we had never prayed for a dog's health before. The episode with the vet lasted several weeks, during which the puppy had to remain for observation and treatment at the animal hospital. The animal's condition was a source of emotional stress for the owner. There were times the owner confessed, that he questioned God as to why would He allow such a dilemma to come upon him?

Eventually God answered the prayer for healing for the dog. He revealed the dog's condition and the correct treatment was able to be ministered to the animal. Meanwhile, the vet maintained e-mail communication with the dog's owner on the dog's progress of recovery. During that time God did something wonderful and supernatural. Not only was the dog healed but the vet's faith in God was being restored. The vet was a backslider in his Christian walk. My friend was totally unaware of that until after the puppy recovered, the vet actually sent him a note of thanks.

He thanked the owner for his witness that moved him to seek and receive restoration in Christ. The owner then realized that in that difficult, emotional period, God had a plan. The vet was being ministered to, during those visits. He was restored into the good Graces of God. Oh! How all of us believers are challenged to stay focused on God amid inexplicable circumstances and to represent Christ wherever we go, for we are *"Ambassadors for Christ."* 2 Cor.5:2 (NKJV)

Therefore, be not ashamed of your testimony of Him. Words have the power to heal, strengthen, encourage, motivate, build and open avenues for deliverance to souls in all forms of captivity. Solomon advises the following in the Book of Proverbs.

"Do not withhold good from those to whom it is due, when it is in your power to do so."
Prov. 3:27 (NKJV)

Therefore, joyfully lift up Jesus wherever you go. Our testimony can be someone else's healing, deliverance or restoration. Every time we witness Jesus' love and saving power to some one else, we are bearing fruit. Never mind if the individual fails to commit his or her life to Christ at that moment. We are to simply sow the seed. One plants, another waters and God gives the increase in His time. Paul says *"I have planted, Apollos watered; but God gave the increase."* 1 Cor. 3:6 (NKJV)

Each time we allow the Holy Spirit in us to nurture the wounded, restore the down- trodden, heal the sick, encourage and strengthen the feeble knees of the weak, give our bread to the poor, intercede for the lost, loose the bands of wickedness through prayer and fasting and edify the body of Christ, we are bearing fruit. When we live by the principles of the word of God, in holiness and righteousness before Him, we are also producing fruit.

When our lives manifest genuine love, joy, peace in the midst of life's storms, goodness, patience in tribulation, faith that moves mountains of doubt and insecurity, longsuffering in dealing with others, meekness, gentleness and temperance, we are bearing fruit. God wants believers to bear continuous fruit. This is all a work of His grace.

> "Go and bear fruit— fruit that will last. Then the Father will give you whatever you ask in my Name."
> Jn 15:16 (NIV)

"Whatever" means anything that is good for you and I; good health, wisdom, understanding, knowledge, revelation, discernment, financial and spiritual prosperity, favor with God and man. In fact, He has promised us all that pertains to life and godliness. Do you want these blessings? Then be about the Father's business.

In the next chapter, we shall examine how Jesus ministered and the pattern that we should follow as we yield ourselves in accomplishing the works of God.

A Prayer of Surrender:

Father, we really want to know you and serve you in ministry in a manner that is pleasing to you. We realize that this is impossible in our own strength, and we are often ignorant of what is your purpose in various circumstances. Grant us the desire, Father and the boldness to tell others about you, even in the face of personal adversity. We thank you in Jesus' Name. Amen.

Chapter 5

The Model Ministry: Jesus

"The Spirit of the Lord is upon me, because He has anointed me, to preach the Gospel to the poor He has sent Me to heal the broken hearted; to proclaim liberty to the captives and recovery of sight to the blind to set at liberty those who are oppressed, to proclaim the acceptable year of the Lord".
Lu. 4:18, 19 (NKJV)

Our Lord Jesus Christ has been the greatest Teacher that has ever traversed this planet on which we live. He knew who He was: His origin, purpose, mission and destiny. We shall consider how He accomplished His mission, and as believers seek to emulate Jesus' example.

*"Most assuredly, I say to you, **He** who believes in Me,*
The works that I do he will do also; and greater works than these he will do, because I go to my Father."
Jn.14:12 (NKJV)

Jesus' purpose in coming to earth is summarized in the scriptures, in the following quotes: He came:

- To seek and to save that which was lost". Lu.4:19b (NKJV)
- To minister and to give His life a ransom for many." Matt. 20:28 (NKJV).
- To destroy the works of the Devil." 1 Jn. 3:8 (NKJV).
- To provide life more abundantly". Jn 10:10 (NKJV). Jesus is referring to believers.

Jesus also came to fulfill the law and the prophets, to give understanding to the written word of God, which was misinterpreted by the Rabbis, Pharisees and other teachers of religious law. He made that clear as he prepared to teach in the Temple on one of the Sabbaths by saying:

"Today this scripture is fulfilled in your hearing." Lu 4:21 (NKJV).

Then He closed the book and taught to the wonder and astonishment of those who were present.

Jesus came to identify Himself with man, though He never sinned, for He would become the substitute offering for atonement of the sins of all mankind. He kept focus on that mission, all the way to His crucifixion on the Cross. Then He said: *"It is finished! And gave up the Ghost"* John 19:30 (KJV). The process was not easy, for Jesus was ostracized. He suffered rejection and opposition from the Pharisees, Sadducees, Scribes, religious leaders, even His own brethren and countrymen, the Jews.

Jesus' Preparation for Ministry

Jesus grew up as a child, participated in Sabbath attendance at worship, worked with His stepfather Joseph, the carpenter and acted as an ordinary citizen of Nazareth until the fullness of time came for His ministry.

In Jesus' day, the Priesthood was administered through the descendants of Aaron. Jesus did not come to earth to destroy the Law, but rather to fulfill it. Jesus was God in Man and came from the priesthood order of Melchizedek (Ps.110:4) and not after Aaron. According to the Levitical System, those who served Aaron's Priesthood had to be consecrated and washed with water. Here is a description of their custom.

> *"He shall put the holy linen tunic and the linen trousers on his body; he shall be girded with a linen tunic*
> *And the linen trousers on his body; he shall be girded with a linen sash, and with the linen turban he shall be attired. These are holy garments. Therefore, he shall wash his body with water, and put them on."*
> Lev: 16:4 (NKJV)

Here is how Jesus satisfied those requirements. Before He began His public Ministry, Jesus came to the Jordan River where He saw sinners being baptized by John unto repentance for the remission of their sins. Jesus requested and was baptized by John. The baptism was equaled to the washing with water and as such met the demands of the Levitical Law for His ministerial work. Jesus also set the example for those who would later believe on Him and He said that the water baptism was *"To fulfill all righteousness.* Matt 3:15 (NKJV).

The baptism was also beneficial to John as well, for God had arranged a special recognition of Jesus at the River Jordon, which He the Father had foretold to John. John saw the Holy Spirit descend on Jesus' head in the form of a dove and rested there awhile. Simultaneously John heard a voice saying,

> *"This is my beloved Son, in whom I am well pleased."*
> Matt. 3:16 (NKJV)

That is the only time in Scripture, that we read of the three personalities of the Godhead appear in congruence. The event gave confirmation to John that Jesus was the Son of God and the one who would come and baptize believers with the Holy Spirit in the future.

Subsequent to Jesus' water baptism, Jesus spent forty days in the wilderness where He was tempted of the Devil in the three key areas of life wherein human beings are tempted: the lust of the flesh, the lust of the eye, and the pride of life. In each case, Jesus quoted the immutable, infallible word of God to defeat the wiles of Satan. We too, will be tempted and must use the same weapon that Jesus used when Satan tempts us to sin or stray away from the call of ministry. For, if Satan could have stopped Jesus from going to the Cross, he would have done so, and the whole world would have been lost. Jesus' victory over the devil warns believers to be on guard against the wiles of the enemy, that temptations and trials will come, but we are *"more than conquerors"* through Christ who strengthens us.

We must recognize Satan as a liar, the Father of all lies and one who has no good thing in Him. He seeks to work overtime in one's imagination, faculty of reasoning, thoughts, memory, and will. He uses fear, doubt, ignorance, procrastination, unforgiveness, anger, frustration, and physical assaults on the body, and whatever he gets a hold on, to hinder God's work.

We, believers must put on the whole armor of God and stand having our loins girded about with truth, which will make us free. We are to wear the breastplate of righteousness, have our feet shod with the preparation of the gospel. Above all, must carry the shield of faith, with which we shall be able to quench the fiery darts of the enemy. We also need the helmet of Salvation and the Sword of the Spirit which is the Word of God that will quench the fiery darts of the enemy. In addition we are to pray all types of prayers, worship and continually give praise to God. The psalmist David says:

> *"Let the high praises of God be in their mouth, and a two-edged sword in their hand, to reap vengeance on the enemy."* Ps 149:6 (NKJV).

The Bible tells us that Jesus returned from the wilderness filled with power of the Holy Spirit. This is the anointing of God. The anointing is the manifestation of the power, presence and personality of God flowing through the human vessel. It destroys every yoke, and bondage of sin, every form of captivity, sickness, and disease.

> *"God anointed Jesus of Nazareth with the Holy Ghost and with power, who went about doing good, and healing all that were oppressed of the devil; for God was with Him."* Acts. 10:38 (NKJV)

All believers are to seek the same anointing like Jesus in order to minister like Jesus did. Jesus traveled to various places where the He perceived that there were needs. So must we. There were times when Jesus went into the synagogue of the Sabbath day. There He preached, taught and ministered healing to sick. Other times He served the needs of people from a boat, a mountain side, a grave yard, in the city street, at a water pool in Bethesda, at a well in Samaria, in homes of publicans and sinners, and public gathering places like a wedding in Cana of Galilee.

Jesus never confined Himself to any one location; He traveled throughout Capernaum, Nazareth, Galilee, Gennesaret, Jerusalem, Tyre and Sidon. His goal was to fulfill the purposes of His anointing. He preached, taught, healed the sick, raised the dead, delivered demoniacs, gave freedom to the oppressed and brought the Gospel of the Kingdom to the poor.

Jesus modeled the Christian life for all to see. He trained twelve men who became His disciples, along with seventy other believers whom He sent out on the trial mission field before going to the Cross. Everything Jesus did was in total agreement with the Father. He said:

> *"I do nothing of myself; but as my Father has taught me,*
> *I speak these things. And he that sent me is with me: The Father hath not left me alone; for I always do those things that please Him."*
> John 8:28b, 29 (NKJV)

Jesus spent quality time with the Father and especially before making decisions. One notable example is, 'choosing His disciples'. He invested time in prayer, even spending all night communicating with the Father.

> *"Now it came to pass in those days that He went out into the mountain to pray and continued all night in prayer to God. And when it was day, He called His disciples to Himself; and from them, He chose twelve whom He also named apostles."*
> Lu.6:12, 13 (NKJV))

Just as how Jesus never depended on Himself, so must all believers always pray for God's guidance in ministry and all other decisions. Jesus encouraged the disciples to

"Ask, and it shall be given to you; seek and you will find;
Knock and it will be opened unto you. For everyone who asks receives, and he who seeks finds and to him who knocks, it will be opened."
Mat. 7:7, 8 (NKJV)

Jesus expects us to ask and keep on asking until the Lord reveals the way to go in ministry. The answer shall be what God sees to be best for us that sometimes may not be what we want to hear or do.

Ministry involves people. Jesus trained, taught, modeled, and developed those disciples with the goal that they would share in His mission, and in the fullness of time, would be prepared and equipped do the same works that Jesus did and even more numerous works after His death on the Cross.

Qualities Jesus Exercised in Ministry

Jesus used opportune moments to teach the disciples' life's principles that they would need to practice for successful living and ministry. He also applied object lessons through simple parables, that none would miss the point of His admonition. Here are the main areas of emphasis.

Authority

By definition, authority is the divine right to act or speak in certain ways in accordance with the power of God. Jesus, received that authority from the Father at the Baptism, through the Holy Spirit (Acts 10:38). He exercised it through the spoken word and the laying on of hands. Jesus calmed the boisterous, raging waves of the sea speaking to the waves:

"'Peace, be still!' He said, and the wind ceased and there was a great calm." Mk. 4:39 (NKJV) emphasis added.

To the man with the withered hand in the synagogue on the Sabbath day, He commanded:

"Stretch forth your hand. And he stretched it out and his hand was restored as whole as the other." Mk. 3:5 (NKJV)

Jesus demonstrated authority over nature, sicknesses, diseases, demoniacs, dumb and deaf spirits and death itself. He commanded deliverance to victims mostly by the power of the word of God. In some cases He touched the victim, like the leper, or Peter's wife's mother, as He rebuked their condition and set them free. At Lazarus' grave He called Lazarus' spirit back from death to life according to the Gospel of St. John 11:43, 44

After Jesus' disciples had been with Him for some time, they had observed the things that Jesus did, and especially how He often prayed before doing many works in the Kingdom, they wanted to be like Jesus, and asked Jesus to teach them to pray. Jesus did. You may read that prayer in Matthew 6:9-13.

In addition, Jesus delegated authority to each of the twelve disciples as is recorded in the following statement.

"He gave them power over unclean spirits, to cast them out, and to heal all manner of sickness and all manner of disease." Matt. 10:21 (NKJV)

He also gave them the keys to kingdom, with power to bind and destroy the works of the enemy, while loosing power and victory in the lives of individuals. He assured them heaven would confirm their efforts that were done in His name.

> *"Verily I say unto you, whatsoever you shall bind on earth,*
> *Shall be bound in heaven and whatsoever you shall lose on earth shall be loosed in heaven."*
> Matt. 28:18 (NKJV)

Jesus sent his disciples on a field trip that would provide them with opportunities to do similar works as He their Master had done. He specifically directed them to go to the lost sheep of the house of Israel, to preach only one message entitled "The Kingdom of Heaven is at hand". They were charged to minister healing to the sick, cleanse the lepers, raise the dead, cast out Demons. As they received freely they were to freely release the power and revelation on the Kingdom of God. (Matt. 10:7, 8) The disciples brought back a great report, fulfilling their assignment.

Humility

Humility is an attitude of lowliness, gentleness, obedience, and total dependence on God and respect for others. It is not egoistic, power seeking or boastful. It is a virtue that is given by God, for God resists the proud and gives grace to the humble. The Bible speaks to believers:

> *"Humble yourselves therefore under the mighty hand of God that He may exalt you in due time."*
> 1 Pet. 5:6 (NKJV)

Jesus had to teach the disciples humility. On one occasion He used a little child and held him up in their midst and taught that except they became as little children they could not enter into the Kingdom of God. Towards the close of Jesus' ministry he began to inform the disciples of his pending visit to Jerusalem, and of the likelihood of his suffering and death. In response two of the disciples, James and John who were brothers asked him to promote them to be chief over the other disciples. They wanted the privilege to sit one on the right and the other on the left hand of Jesus in the future of his kingdom. Immediately Jesus rebuked them and taught the principle that 'to be chief is to be a servant' which is a humbling experience to many. Jesus further demonstrated humility by washing the disciples' feet at the last supper as an example for posterity. We are to wash one another's feet. Finally, the whole act of Jesus' coming and bringing salvation to the human race is a complete act of humility.

> *"And found in the fashion of a man, he humbled himself, and became obedient to the point of death, even the death of the cross. Therefore God also has highly exalted Him and given Him a name that is above every name."* Phil. 2:8 (NKJV)

This position is one of power and glory. As every believer humbles himself continually before the Almighty God, he or she will receive the necessary understanding, revelation and wherewithal to graciously minister in the kingdom of God.

Compassion

Compassion is an act of care and sympathy usually shown in deeds of kindness and consideration to others in any kind of difficulty or crisis. The disciples lacked this virtue. They seemed not to have fully comprehended Jesus' mission and at some point tried to put barriers hoping to prevent the desperate from getting to Jesus. The story is told of a Syro-Phoencian Woman, a Gentile, who had crossed cultural and religious lines to get to where Jesus was. She worshipped Him from a distance crying out:

> *"Have mercy on me, O Lord, Son of David! My daughter is severely demon-possessed... Lord help me!"* Matt. 15: 22b, 25b (NKJV)

The disciples tried to silence her, urging Jesus to send her away. A dialogue followed between Jesus and this mother, upon which when Jesus saw her faith, He healed the daughter. Jesus also showed compassion for the multitude who followed Him for days and had nothing to eat. He miraculously increased a few loaves and fishes to feed thousands of people in a dessert place. He took the little children in His arms and blessed them, when the disciples wanted to send them away. Jesus' heart was full of compassion and all who would minister need to imitate Him.

Love

Love in the unconditional caring and devotion that we show to others. Jesus required this of the disciples and everyone who accepts Him as their Savior and Lord as well. We are to love one another and so fulfill the law. Ministry must flow from a genuine heart of love. It is love that took Jesus to the cross to pay the price of the sins of the entire world. He said.

> *" A new commandment I give unto you, that you love one another; as I have loved you, that you also love one another. By this all will know that you are My disciples, if you have love for one another."*
> Jn. 13:34, 35 (NKJV)

Commitment

Commitment is a state of personal dedication to someone, or a cause which results in actively promoting and working for their well-being. Commitment requires faith, diligence, availability and self denial. Serious commitment leaves no room for options. Instead there is an increase in steadfastness, determination and focus on obtaining the prize or established goals. Commitment includes some measure of sacrifice to please God, serve Him and receive the 'crown of righteousness' that is laid up for the over-comers. Jesus taught His disciples:

> *"If anyone desires to come after Me, let him deny himself, and take up his cross and follow Me. For whoever desires to save his life, will lose it, but whoever loses his life, for my sake, will find it.*
> Matt. 16: 24 (NKJV)

This means a total surrender of one's self to the will of God. To one potential disciple who requested to be allowed to go and burry his father first before becoming a disciple Jesus taught the lesson on separation unto Him. He said: *"Let the dead bury their dead, but come and follow me."* This also suggests there's no proverbial looking back for those who look back are considered to be unfit for the Kingdom of God. It is a life for a life and the development of a spiritual discipline.

God enters into a covenant with believers who are committed to Him. He honors and fulfils every aspect of that covenant to the measure that believers become rooted and grounded in Him, look unto Him the author and finisher of their faith, stand on His promises that are sure, live by the precepts and power of His word and obey Him in service to Him. Believers are not alone, just as the disciples were not alone for Jesus was with them, so the angels are with us (Ps. 34:7) and Jesus is within us in the personality of the Holy Spirit. *"Lo I am with you always, even to the end of the age. Amen."* Matt. 28:20b (NKJV)

A Prayer of Thanksgiving

Father thank you for sending your only begotten Son Jesus Christ to die for us, so we can be saved, come to know you and learn how to effectively minister in your kingdom. Thank you for placing your unconditional love in our hearts that we may love you and one another. We are challenged by Christ's example to be disciples, sharing the same love we have received from you with others, and meeting the needs of others through your guidance, wisdom and grace. Teach us how to remain steadfast, faithful and obedient to this call that your kingdom work will be advanced and we ask this in Jesus' Name. Amen.

Chapter 6

Personal Preparation to Minister

"Consider one another in order to stir up love and good works." Heb. 10:24 (NKJV)

Imagine you or I have an important event coming up within the next two days. We would most likely make preparations in advance of our participation. If travel is involved, that would be arranged. We would also consider the nature of the appointment and equip ourselves with any tools we think we might need. In other words we would do our homework and position ourselves to get the maximum benefit from the encounter. All truth is parallel. As it is in the natural, so it is in the spiritual. Launching out into ministry requires personal preparation. Let us consider some pre-requisites.

The minister needs to be equipped with the anointing of the Holy Spirit and power. Power is derived from the Greek word *dunamis* meaning 'brute force and ability'. Within the anointing lie all the wisdom, discernment and attributes of God that a minister will need. Wisdom is good judgment, discernment, divine intelligence, understanding and depth of insight that are transmitted into our spirit by the Holy Spirit. Discernment is the supernatural ability to perceive by revelation what is often hidden to the naked eye. The attributes of

God are his righteousness, holiness, justice, judgment, love, peace, grace, mercy, wisdom, knowledge and understanding. Remember, Jesus was anointed for ministry (Acts 10:38). He demonstrated the attributes of God, and so must everyone, who seeks to conform to the image of Christ and continue the works that Jesus did before going to the Cross for the entire world's redemption.

There is a specific anointing for each area of ministry (i.e. preaching, teaching, healing, witness, intercession etc.). Be sure to seek the Lord in prayer for the anointing, and then wait before Him for that blessing before taking matters into your own hands. Some people testify that the anointing comes upon them like a feeling of electricity passing through their bodies. Others say, it is like a surge of heat passing through them and yet others express the sensation as a blanket of over shadowing peace on them. You will know when the anointing is release on you, for surely the Holy Spirit does not want His partners to be ignorant of His presence and work.

Ministry is service to others with the kingdom of God in mind. It often involves warfare with an opponent who is bent on hindering and often destroying God's interests in the earth. Satan is the Prince of the power of the air, the enemy of all Righteousness. He controls a highly organized system of disembodied demonic forces established in heavenly places. Jesus defeated him at the cross over 2,000 years ago yet he is not bound and exerts his influence on those who do not know Jesus nor understand the importance of His finished work at the cross. They are ignorant of the power Jesus has given to His followers to overcome the work of the enemy. Ministers are warned to wear the whole armor that God has specifically designed and tailor made for each person. The fact is that God knows every believer's weakness and His potential for our lives; we should never overlook or omit any part of the armor that Paul described in his letter to the Church at Ephesus. He said:

"Stand firm with the belt of truth, buckled under the waist with the breast-plate of righteousness in place. With your feet fitted with the readiness that comes from the gospel of peace. In addition to all this, taking the shield of faith with which you can extinguish all the flying arrows of the devil.
Take the helmet of salvation, which is the sword of the Spirit, which is the word of God. And pray in the Spirit and on all occasions with all kinds of prayers and requests. With this in mind, be alert and always praying for the saints". Eph. 6:14-18 (NIV)

If we neglect any part of the outfit, that area serves as an open door for the assaults of the devil in attacking whether our finances, health, employment, business, marriage, or the welfare of close family members. To counteract this evil, God has given tools of warfare that are mighty through Him for the demolishing of the strongholds of the adversary. By strongholds we refer to well fortified areas that resist dismantling. They can be compared to bunkers or fortresses. Satan establishes these strongholds in the minds of individuals and so controls their behavior. The list of the weapons for warfare includes:

Prayer

Prayer is the muscle that moves the hand of God. John Wesley said "God does nothing, but in answer to prayer." The more prayer then, the greater the ministry's potential for victory.

Fasting

This is abstinence usually from food and pleasures over a period of time as someone seeks God and His will. Fasting empowers prayers, produces greater spiritual freedom and releases spiritual gifts and guidance for ministry. Fasting also looses bands of wickedness, destroys yokes of bondage and liberates captives of oppression. Many healings and deliverances are accompanied with fasting. Jesus taught His disciples that certain types of deliverances are only wrought through prayer and fasting (Matt. 7:21)

Praise and Worship

Praise welcomes the presence of God in our midst, glorifies God and confounds the enemy. This destroys the devil's schemes. Worship releases favor from God and the manifestation of victory.

The Word

The word is powerful, sharp as a two-edged sword cutting and separating right from wrong, truth from error, and discerning the intent of the hearts of others. We must believe and constantly apply the word in prayer, confessing what it says about the situation under consideration, and releasing our faith for the answer.

The Name of Jesus

His Name is the power of attorney to do damage to Satan's plans. It is by obedience and faith in the name of Jesus shall all ministries be fulfilled.

Personal Confession

There is power in the tongue. We are to speak with authority, and our words are to declare the will of God as understood in the scriptures. Let us be careful to avoid uttering vain and doubtful words which produce instability. James writes that the double minded individual receives nothing from the Lord (James 1: 8). We are to allow the Holy Spirit to give the unction to speak. In other words we must stay connected to the Holy Spirit. Jesus said: *"If you remain in me and my words remain in you, ask whatever you wish, and it will be given you."* Jn.15:7 (NIV)

God desires that we produce much fruit for that brings Him glory. Fruit embodies healings, witnessing, deliverances, restoration and teaching, the manifestation of His love, joy, peace, long-suffering, goodness, faith, gentleness, meekness and self control in our lives.

We have been made one with the Father and Jesus through the Holy Spirit and Jesus' priestly prayer. (Jn. 7:21). This connection is to be maintained through worship, prayer, meditating on the word, waiting before God and obeying His commands. We are to be very careful not to allow the tyranny of the urgent to trick us into making decisions that are void of the God's council. When we realize that our schedule over shadows our time with God, we need to rethink what is happening, repent and be restored; for without Jesus, we cannot accomplish anything for the kingdom. It can be compared to having a car and trying to run it without gas or oil. That would totally destroy the engine that gives life to the vehicle. As we remain connected to the vine who is Jesus, we will produce much desirable fruit for the Kingdom.

In ministering, some tasks appear to be more daunting than others. In each case, we need to know and confess who we are in Christ. We are what the word says about us. Jesus knew His identity and so must we. We have a covenant relationship with God who keeps His word. We are called, chosen and appointed ambassadors of Christ on a mission here on earth, for the Kingdom of God, to fulfill the word of God (Col. 1:26b). We are not alone, for the angel of God encamps with us to deliver us (Ps.34:7), so is Jesus our Intercessor and Redeemer (Col.1:27); and the Holy Spirit, our *paraclete or 'helper'*. (Matt.28:20b).

Ministers as Ambassadors

In daily living, an ambassador represents an entity – typically a government, its plans, rules, and philosophy. That individual speaks on behalf of that government at all times and exhibits interest in the concerns of that sovereignty. He or she also has certain privileged rights and access to the ruling authority of that country more so than other ranking citizen. In spiritual matters believers have a similar role as ambassadors of Christ. He, that is, Christ has given each of us power in the anointing and authority in Jesus' Name, to preach the good news of the gospel, to witness to unbelievers, to lift up the down-trodden, heal the sick and broken hearted, deliver captives, to encourage and restore the faint-hearted, that they may become trees of righteousness - the planting of our God. Ambassadors also have the privilege of being advocates for souls and represent God's interests in the earth.

As we refresh our minds on Jesus' model for the ministry, we notice that Jesus surrounded Himself with help mostly from the disciples. When it was time for ministry, He dispatched them in groups of two. It takes two parties to agree on a matter and there is power in agreement. God promises to answer requests that are offered in agreement to Him in heaven (Matt. 28:19). It is also written in the scriptures that one can put 1,000 demons to flight and two can put 10,000 to flight according to Deuteronomy 32:30. Everyone needs a prayer covering for ministry, and a prayer partner as that person ministers. Ask the Holy Spirit to reveal such a person and proceed to foster that relationship.

It is also very important to be led by the Holy Spirit in ministry. This requires that our minds be free of prejudices, self-righteousness, wrong attitudes, judgmental spirits, jealousies, anger, malice and human wisdom. We have to pray and spend quality time in the presence of the Lord; to repent and cleanse our spirit through the power of the Blood of Christ. *"Be clean, you who bear that bear the vessels of the LORD."* Is. 52:11 (NKJV)

It is essential that we cultivate a listening ear; to have the patience to listen to the 'seeker' without entertaining personal negative emotions; to reach out and ask God for His guidance in meeting the particular needs to be addressed. Sometimes it may be difficult to minister in a particular area, if we are either ignorant of what to do, or have personal struggles in that area. No one is perfect and that is one reason why it is good to have another person working with us to assist as we minister.

The Holy Spirit will not take us where He will not sustain us and He will be to us just what we allow Him to be. He prepares us for the unexpected and the unusual as we spend time in prayer ahead of ministering. I have found that in some areas, it has been helpful for me to ask the seeker, to relate his needs that we can establish agreement in ministry. Jesus did a similar thing and He is our model. Blind Bartimaeus is such an example that we read about in Mark (10:51, 52). Jesus stirred this blind man's faith to believe for his miracle.

Unity in the Spirit is vital to produce favorable results in ministry. Be not afraid to be selective regarding the support staff chosen to get a job successfully completed. Everyone does not have faith. Jesus mobilized three of His disciples to be with Him as He raised Jairus' daughter from the dead. He dismissed the spectators as we find in Matthew (9:23-25). We are to imitate Jesus, for we have the mind of Christ.

A Prayer of Preparation

Father thank you for the model Jesus has left us and for the assurance that as we embark on the ministry you are with us at every point. We are moving forward in obedience to the call and anointing on our lives. Please grant to us understanding and discernment as we minister to others. Help us to rightly use your tools of service in ministry. Be our counselor and strength always. Guide us to those people and resources we need to effectively minister. We want to bring much glory to your name and bear fruit for the Kingdom. In Jesus' Name I pray. Amen.

Chapter 7

Going Forth in Ministry

"And I, if I be lifted up from the earth will draw all men peoples to myself". Jn. 12:32 (NKJV)

Ministering to New Believers

The born again experience legitimizes all believers to become sons of God, kingdom citizens, and joint heirs with Christ (Jn.1:12, Rom. 8:17). They have been translated from the kingdom of darkness that is controlled by Satan, into the kingdom of light in Jesus Christ (Col. 1:13).

Just as newborn infants need to be nurtured, taught and trained to develop into healthy productive individuals, so also must new believers receive opportunities for healthy growth and maturity. It is doubtful to think that without instruction, divine protection and guidance, they will be able to escape the vulnerable effects of exposure to legalism, traditionalism, occultism, deception, confusion and error. New believers need to be assured of their salvation. The experience is intended to be more than a conversion or change in heart. It is to be a complete spiritual make over or transformation by the renewing of the mind in the Word. When the reality of this is understood and accepted, the Holy Spirit brings individuals into experiences whereby they may come into the knowledge of the acceptable will of God for their lives. (Rom.12:2)

The mind is the seat of the emotions, the reservoir of fears, worries, disappointments, disillusionment, diminished hopes, shattered dreams, self destructive behaviors and damaged self-esteem. It is the storage place of anger, jealousies and rebellion. It controls the faculties of reasoning, memory, imagination, conscience and affections. Many who are saved today testify that Christ's salvation rescued them from the mental and emotional depravity of their mind.

Experience has taught me that in ministering to new believers, individually or in a group that they want to understand salvation, to be healed from their past concerns and the unpleasant memories, to learn how to pray and develop relationship with God and to have their self esteem restored. They want to get to really know God, His plans for their new life and to be taught how to win the battles of temptation brought on by the enemy.

Foremost, as a minister one needs to be a good listener, to be non-judgmental, to exercise some patience and be transparent as well. People need to know the person ministering is open, sincere, vulnerable in their humanity, not hypocritical, but a vessel that God wants to use to bring help in their need. As I listen to new Christians, I seek the Holy Spirit for His enlightenment on how to address their needs. I want to know, what Jesus would do if He were physically present, and to serve their needs in a similar manner.

Occasionally God allows me to give a short testimony of how I came to know and accept Jesus into my life. I would express some of my feelings that were similar to those they related, and how by the marvelous love and grace of God, I have come through thus far to be able to declare to them that they too can make it, if they would follow on to know the Lord. We discuss the social implications of their decisions - that they may loose friends and associates, as I did, but that God would give them new friends and associates in the body of Christ. I use the issues and concerns for prayer focus before closing the time together.

I introduce the Bible to them as their road map for life in Christ. The Word must be their daily food, as it is essential for spiritual survival, growth and maturity. Invariably, everyone is encouraged and assigned the Gospel of John for their daily reading and personal Bible Study. This book bears the best presentation of Jesus Christ, the incarnate Word, the Son of the Living God and the only redeemer for man's soul. He is Eternal Life (Jn. 17:3) and gives assurance by His very own words that cannot lie (Heb 6:18), that whosoever comes to Him, He will raise them up at the last day (Jn. 6:44). Jesus is the Bread of Life; His Word supplies the daily spiritual nourishment for the soul. His indwelling presence in the believer is strengthened because of the Word. Hence, the greater the intake of the word and obedience to its instructions, the greater is the potential for the Holy Spirit to manifest His internal supernatural control. He is the power that renews the mind and enables a Christian to think and act differently than he or she would in the past. Jesus said:

"It has been written, man shall not live and be upheld and sustained by bread alone, but by every word that comes forth from the mouth of God."
Matt. 4:4 (AMP)

I encourage new believers to fellowship around the Bible, scripture memorization, prayer and other spiritual activities and conversations. As the Holy Spirit develops their understanding, we use the scriptures for their guidance in dealing with the issues that they have raised. Discoveries in the word of God often expose the need for repentance and/or forgiveness of others as pre-requisites for healing. We often share steps we can take to build bridges of love in our relationships that would replace walls of isolation. Sometimes this close contact ministry lasts about two months, so as to strengthen new believers in their faith and help them to understand the word and nature of God.

A testimony is a very effective tool to be used in building faith in others who are seeking to find themselves in God. God gets glory every time we testify. It's another way to bear fruit, as we are also edifying the hearers and stirring up their faith so they too might receive the blessings of the Lord by faith. We as ministers continue to overcome through our testimonies.

Ministering to God

God loves the fellowship of His sons and daughters. He created us for worship and fellowship. That practice began back in the Garden of Eden with Adam and Eve. It was a daily meeting time and place in the Garden of Eden until sin deceived the couple. Sin has always been the wedge that separates our connection with the Father. God is Holy and does not co-exist with sinful practices. A great way to begin in ministry is to commit to a life of daily devotion to God. This includes prayer, bible reading, meditation and worship. I encourage you to plan a special time and place in your home to meet for your special time with God. This will prevent distractions, interruptions and conflicts. It should be a time when you can focus on the Lord. Perhaps it is early in the morning before daybreak or late at night. I like the early morning for my mind is rested and the thinking is clear. Bring a notebook and writing tool to your special meeting place.

Begin the session with prayer, which is, a simple conversation to God. Praise Him, honor Him for who He is, and thank Him for the many blessings including salvation and the desire to be with Him in this time of devotion. Ask Him to draw you closer to Him and to reveal Himself and His ways to you in the time of fellowship. Just think of it, you will be cultivating a habit like Jesus our model.

> *"Very early in the morning while it was still dark, Jesus got up, left His house and went off into a solitary place where he prayed."* Mk. 1:35 (NIV)

Prayer gets God's attention and He will minister to your needs as you draw near to Him.

> *"You will seek me and find me, when you seek me with your whole heart. I will be found of you"*, declares the Lord". Jer. 29:13 (NIV)

As you begin your Bible reading, it is a good practice to read the passage slowly and perhaps twice. Think on what the passage is saying to you. Use your notebook to record your thoughts. The word comes to instruct us in righteousness, therefore, determine if the passage is revealing any sins you need to forsake, any promises that you can claim; any warning for which you are to take special heed and finally any teaching about Jesus, God and the Holy Spirit for you to grasp.

Make a note of all these things for your reflections and endeavor by His grace to accomplish them. Devotion time can be a most wonderful experience with the Lord. It enriches your life. The more quiet time spent in His presence, the greater the victories and transformation into the image of Christ. Instead of worrying, your spirit is bathed with peace, as you experience the love and grace of God. Sometimes you even hear His voice speaking to you. God wants all His children to know Him and to recognize His voice.

What happens when despite following a protocol, someone struggles with devotion and bible reading? I believe this happens where there are unresolved issues, or over busy schedules in that person's life that need to be addressed. The individual needs to bring every emotion and /or abuse to the cross, to forgive and release any inward pain, so as to gain the peace and joy in the Lord. Forgiveness is the key that opens the door to mercy and grace. We must forgive others and ourselves as well to be able to experience this peace.

Sometimes there are undesirable habits that are difficult to get rid of. For example an undisciplined tongue, bad temper, credit card abuse etc. It is here that fasting and prayer will be necessary to destroy those strongholds created by such habits, and to give the freedom and deliverance that are needed to effectively witness to others on the power of God to do similar things in their lives. Fasting brings the body under subjection to the power of God and establishes the Lordship of Christ in a person's life. Jesus did it, and He is our model. The Bible says that after Jesus' fasting was complete, that returned from the Wilderness being filled with the power of the Holy Ghost to heal, deliver, and work miracles and to save individuals. We can all benefit from such experience.

Ministering Within the Body of Christ

The Holy Spirit so wants us to minister to each other's needs within the church, that He inspired Paul to include this command in his letter to the church at Galatia. Here is what he writes:

> *"Brethren, if any person is overtaken in misconduct or sin of any sort, you who are spiritual [who are responsive to and controlled by the Spirit] should set him right and restore and reinstate him, without any sense of superiority and with all gentleness, keeping an attentive eye on yourself, lest you should*

be tempted also. Bear (endure, carry) one another's burdens and troublesome moral faults, and in the way fulfill and observe perfectly the law of Christ (the Messiah) and complete what is lacking [in your obedience to it]"* Gal.6: 1, 2 (AMP)

Let us note however, that the mandate is given to a specific group of believers, namely, those who are responsive and controlled by the Holy Spirit. This is not just to a person who has the Holy Spirit, but to the one who hears, understands and obeys the Holy Spirit. You will also notice that there is a warning to first protect yourself as you go forth to minister. If a person attempts to minister in the absence of the anointing and wisdom, he can end up being a victim. Ministry involves confronting the forces of darkness and the enemy will put up a fight before releasing his victim. Spending time in the presence of the Lord before entering the battle ground with the enemy is vital.

It is obvious that the manifestation of certain behaviors in individuals give clues to evil spirits that are oppressing and controlling them and just as a tree is known by the fruit it produces (Matt. 7:2, NKJV) so it is, that the trained minister can identify the spirits motivating abnormal behaviors manifested in individuals. For example, a person who keeps on telling falsehood and tries to deceive or defraud others is controlled by a lying spirit. Similarly, spirits of pride, fear, infirmity, loneliness, seduction, perversion etcetera are exposed, identified and destroyed through the power of the Holy Spirit and the blood of Jesus.

Whenever I minister to the Body of Christ, my focus is to present Jesus and all He is as declared in the inerrant, infallible word of God and as experienced through daily victories. Every testimony about Him releases His power to meet similar needs in those who receive the testimony.

> *"Whoever confesses that Jesus is the Son of God, God lives in him, and he in God.* 1 Jn 4:14 (NKJV)
>
> *"We have this treasure in earthen vessels that the excellence of the power may be of God and not of us."* 2Cor. 4:5 (NKJV)
>
> *"No good thing will He withhold from those who walk uprightly."* Ps. 84:11 (NKJV)

In preparing and officiating in ministry I seek to fully acknowledge who I am by confession and absolute dependence on the Lord. I am an Ambassador of Christ on assignment; anointed with power and authority to speak as the oracle of God. By revelation, I declare God's truth, His will, plan and purposes to believers for that particular time and season. I am His possession and not my own. The words I speak must be given in love and humility.

I am also made cognizant of any spiritual forces in the environment. Such forces are intended to distract and maintain their illegal preoccupation and dominion over the minds of the hearers. God has given me spiritual weapons to destroy the strongholds of the enemy and to take captive every thought or imagination that exalts itself against the word of God. Every action I take is to be Spirit-led, just like Jesus was in His ministry. He is model, mentor, anointing, guide and shield. I am not alone. He, the Father and the ministering angel are with me and I get assurance when I think of such passages of scripture as:

> *"Fear not, for I have redeemed you; I have summoned you, by name; you are mine; when you pass through the waters,*
> *I will be with you; and when you pass through the rivers,*

They will not sweep over you. When you walk through the fire, you will not be burned; the flames will not set you ablaze. For I am the Lord, you God, the holy one of Israel, your Savior; do not be afraid, for I am with you." Is.43:1b-3a, 5a (NIV)

"No weapon forged against you will prevail, and you will refute every tongue that accuses you. This is the heritage of the servants of the Lord, and this is their vindication from me, declares the Lord."
Is. 54:17 (NIV)

"You must go to everyone I send you and a say whatever I command you. Do not be afraid of them, for I am with you and will rescue you. Declares the Lord. Now I have put my words into your mouth.
Jer. 1: 7b, 8, 9b (NIV)

Opportunities for ministry present themselves almost daily and through many avenues. The telephone, letter writing, one to one contacts, home cell groups and other community activities, seminars, prayer sessions, hospital visitation - preaching and teaching are but to name a few. Each encounter is different but is designed to glorify God, to establish His kingdom on earth, to expose and destroy the works of Satan. Captives are liberated, healed, restored, and delivered. The believers are edified and appropriately challenged to love and good works. I believe as we freely receive of the favor of God for our needs, we are to freely bless others for the same. Therefore, if someone has been healed or delivered, he or she should both testify and minister healing prayers for someone else who has that or similar need. I will share instances I have experienced in ministry.

Ministering to the Spiritually Oppressed

Some time ago, a believer asked me to come and offer prayers in her home. She claimed that her sleep at night would be often interrupted by an evil presence in her room. She further said that she had occasionally seen a silhouette moving in her home and that she needed help to pray and dispel that spirit from her home. In response, I sought the Lord and He directed me to engage two mature anointed pray warriors to accompany me in the encounter. We prepared ourselves, in prayer and the word - being mindful to put on the whole armor of God, to cover ourselves with the blood of Jesus before entering the home.

This home was decorated with figurines and artifacts. We sang songs on the power of the Blood of Jesus Christ, read some scriptures including Ps. 27:1-5; Ps. 91:1-13 and confessed that everything that our heavenly Father had not authorized in that home had to desist its activity, and leave in Jesus' Name. We anointed each room, drove out unclean spirits through the blood of Jesus, declared blessings and invited the holy presence of God to abide there.

We then prayed for the owner, that God would bless her with assurance of His peace, and protection; that He would give her wisdom in protecting her home, and revelation of His power in her to maintain a spiritually clean house. We asked the Lord to release an angel on assignment to the home to ward off any assaults of evil. She has since then been very happy and has testified of peace in her home.

It may be helpful for the reader to understand that in the unseen world, evil spirits can be released in your homes through the types of television programs, the nature of music and certain artifacts you allow in your homes. We have seen it in the increase of violence exhibited by regular viewers of violent film and television. Music definitely releases spirits. Moods are set by to type of music to which a person listens. In the Bible David played anointed music on a harp which had the effect of driving out the evil, distressing spirit that was on Saul (1 Sam. 16:23). If anointed music has that power, it is not difficult to comprehend the opposing effect that some other types of music can have in seducing people to act out the lyrics and mood the song presents.

I believe that from time to time we should spiritually clean our houses. You get rid of figurines, trinkets and charms for they attract spirits, sanctify your home with prayer and devotional music. Sometimes you may need to leave the word of God on CD or inspirational music playing all day in your homes and invite the fragrance of the anointing of the Holy Spirit to maintain its saturation in your dwelling.

Ministering to the Violated and Victimized

A mature Christian woman sustained a house break one night, while she was at work. The perpetrator forced his entry through the main entrance door. The victim felt violated. Her home was totally ransacked and some heavy equipment left inoperable. She was unable to determine her losses and was scared the burglar might attempt to return – given the lack of a suitable door.

As I received the telephone call and listened, I felt the anxiety and fear in her complaint. While she spoke, I interceded for the peace of God to manifest His presence and to control her inner man. When it was my turn to speak, I empathized with the situation and continued to find out the steps she had taken thus far to involve law enforcement. Then I began to remind her of God's love and power to provide for her needs. Through the help of the Holy Spirit, she was able to see how God had convened it for her to be away at work for things could have been worse if the attacker had found her at home. The goodness of the Lord endures forever!

We identified the spirits of fear and anxiety as messengers of Satan, that were sent to oppress her spirit, steal her peace and hinder her devotions to God. She was encouraged to focus on the indwelling presence of the Holy Spirit, who was waiting to meet her need. Realizing, her struggle I read Psalms 46 and 91.

> *"Faith comes by hearing and hearing by the word of God."* Rom. 10:17 (NKJV)

Then we agreed in prayer for God to supernaturally touch her emotions and give her His peace in the midst of this storm. We covered the home in prayer – calling on the blood of Jesus, and asked for an angel to be dispatched on assignment at the entrance of the home, warding off any assaults of the enemy. The prayer intervention brought results. The process of the physical property protection and restoration would take several days. However, the power and presence of God sustained this woman during the entire trial. The Lord fulfils his promises in His word. He said that he would send His angels to encamp about all who fear Him and to deliver them from all their trouble. We claimed that promise and this scripture:

> *"You (the Lord Jesus) will keep him in perfect peace, whose mind is stayed on you, because he trusts in you."* Is. 26:3 (NKJV)

A follow up call later revealed how God provided for the total restoration of the home. Her son arrived from out of state and took care of managing the repairs. She has since being challenged to become an intercessor for the deliverance and/ or salvation for the soul of the home invader. One does not know why the Lord allows bad things to happen to His children at times, but we believe that when we are complacent about the wrong behaviors of others, we are less likely to seek the Lord or become concerned for their salvation. God sent Jesus to redeem the whole world. His disciples are to seek to get others saved and delivered like Jesus did. Everyone needs Jesus. The victim in this case had to get past the hurt and reach the point to release forgiveness of the intruder. Only then, would she manifest the mind of Christ, and her prayers be heard in heaven on the invader's behalf. David expressed this truth in the Psalms where he wrote:

"I cried unto him with my mouth; his praise was on my tongue. If I had cherished sin in my heart, the Lord would not have listened; but God has surely listened and heard my voice in prayer."
(Ps.66:16-19 NIV)

Ministering to Broken Relationships

Forgiveness gives spiritual freedom and destroys the sting of the offense. The victim is made free to love, pray, praise, think, to be restored and to help someone else going who might be going through a similar situation. When this happens God is really pleased. The outcome is the fruit of righteousness for which God is glorified and we will be in alignment with His divine plan.

Some time ago a young married Christian couple was going through difficult situations associated with loyalty, respect, intervention of extended family and stress. They requested prayer and asked me to be a listening and helpful ear. As I listened the Holy Spirit led me to have the husband and the wife each to separately write down the things that drew them together in marriage. Then each was to write down what he or she enjoyed about the other. Next each was to list the things that caused displeasure in the other partner. The three sets of information were used to: highlight the good in each person, to expose the imperfections as a means of balance and to identify ungodly behaviors. They agreed to repent of unhealthy behaviors, insensitivities to each other's needs and ask for each other's forgiveness. The Holy Spirit ministered to their needs as we prayed and discussed the Word relevant for their situation. They both agreed to the steps each was to conscientiously observe in order to sustain their healing and spiritual maturity as a family. There is power in forgiveness. To this day, the family is doing well and the children are growing up with respect. We must always remember the thief comes to steal, kill and destroy but God sent Jesus to bring life and that more abundantly and there is nothing too hard for God to do.

Ministering Physical Healing

The Lord has shown Himself to be the God of miracles for today. About several months ago, a friend's unborn grandchild was developing abnormally in the mother's womb. Some of the intestines were growing outside the child's body. We sought the Lord in intercession knowing He is the Almighty, ever Powerful Omniscient God. We clearly asked Him for a miracle, worshipped Him and kept thanking Him as the time went by. God heard our prayers and the infant was born normal. Our God is awesome! He will be to us just what we let Him to be. He will be a father providing for every need in according to His abundant riches in glory. He is a friend who sticks closer than any brother. He is a healer for He created every tissue, muscle, organ and system of our body, and by His stripes we are healed. God never fails. Let Him be your miracle-worker and your all in all.

Ministering Through Physical Limitation

In 1995 I sustained a fracture to my left ankle as I fell on the glazed, icy-covering on my driveway one late evening. For several months following the incident, I was unable to walk, while the cast on my leg secured the alignment of bone tissues for healing to my foot. I had much time to reflect on my life and walk with the Lord. I believed my fracture was the result of being out of the will of God.

Sometimes we are self-willed and inconsistent with our commitments to God. We grow lackadaisical in our prayer life, witness and in mortifying the deeds of our flesh. God certainly got my attention while I was incapacitated at home. I presented myself at his mercy seat, repented, sought his forgiveness, restoration, physical and emotional healing. He rekindled my zeal for Him and His word. It was during that time that I was able to focus on the reality that I was the first and the only one among my siblings to give my life to Christ and that the Lord wanted me to witness His saving Grace to those siblings who were overseas.

God anointed me to produce an audiotape a monologue that I sent to each of my two brothers in the United Kingdom. A year later I took a copy for my sister on a visit to London. In the fullness of time God saved my sister, and this is her testimony:

> "Today, I joyfully give my testimony of how I received Jesus Christ as my Lord and Savior. It was in 1996 that my sister visited London from Boston and brought me a Bible. It was the New International Version Study Bible. She also brought an audiotape that she said was made personally for me. The tape contained a message entitled "The Way to God". At that time I was preoccupied with night clubs on weekends and participating in whatever wiles that

the world had to offer. Therefore, receiving the Bible and tape at that time did not mean much to me; I had no understanding of the concept of what was in the Bible.

One day I was home alone and felt like playing the tape. I played it once, then again, and again. There was something about that tape. I played in the car and even felt a need to hear it again at bedtime. Something was happening to me; something began to yield in me. I got the Bible and started praying to God in the name of Jesus Christ our Lord, and I asked God to teach me to read the Word with the Spirit's understanding that comes through Jesus Christ.

God heard my prayer. My heart was so burdened with the disappointment, mistrust, frustration, anger and unforgiveness towards others. I had lost the joy to even smile. I said, 'God I know in me there is joy but I am unable to express it. I feel like I am in a bottle with a lid on it, like champagne locked in a bottle needing to come out.' Not long after, God answered that prayer when, in 2000, Unknown to me, my children arranged a surprise trip for me to visit the United States. There was nothing left undone. I was re-united with my sister in Boston for three weeks. The trip was life-changing for me with unforgettable memories; for in my sister's home, I would come to surrender my life and receive the greatest gift of eternal life in Jesus.

This is how it happened. My sister spoke about Jesus in the word after which I allowed her to pray for me. As she held my hands and prayed I felt a shiver like electricity go through my entire body and uncontrollable tears flowed from my eyes. It was then that I invited Jesus to take over my life.

Something supernatural happened to me I cannot explain. That night I was awakened about 3:00am and remained awake until about 6:00am. I had an experience with God. Something took place. I was fully aware but motionless. I could only lay and watch the experience which confirmed for me that God is real. Jesus came and sorted me out and brought me a new beginning. He gave me joy and laughter and I will never be the same again.

Since then, He has filled me with the Holy Spirit and has revealed Himself to me. He has been shown me His counsel in His word for the problems of life. He has been showing how to witness to my family members. He has saved one daughter and filled her with the Holy Spirit and is drawing the other to Him. I praise Him! He is the best thing that has ever happened to me."

Wow! What a testimony of the greatness of our God. His ways are past finding out but are revealed as we walk with Him. His timing is so different from ours. I give Him all the glory for saving my sister and members of my family. I hold unto the promise that if I walk uprightly before Him, there will be no good thing that He would withhold from me. My request before Him is that He will save all my family members.

If you are saved and have unsaved loved ones for whom you have been praying and witnessing, be encouraged and remain consistent in living the life that honors the Savior, before them. Shower them with *'agape'* love and in the fullness of time, God will bring them into the salvation experience and kingdom living.

Ministering to Ministers

Ministers serve but there are times when we need to be served. Sometimes we may be caught off guard. The cares of living, disobedience to the Holy Spirit, self-will can be the culprits. We can become lackadaisical in maintaining communion, worship of the Father, and even sacrifice the consistency in their prayer life. The enemy will attack us unaware, especially if the rigors of schedule and deadlines drain us of adequate time with God. We become workers for God instead workers with God. Satan loves to attack our health and finances which provide for ministry to others.

A minister friend of mine was working overtime in ministering to others. His assignments would take several hours crossing the state many days each week. Then he would minister to all types of needs often on a one on one basis. God gave him continuous victories and volumes of prayer requests. With his schedule, he hardly slept at times. He suddenly became very ill.

Although he had prayer partners praying for him, the enemy attacked his physical body with a vengeance. Daily continuous intercession was made on his behalf. Friends included a fast for his health. I recall sending short prayers and scripture quotes to his voicemail for days before he had the energy to respond. A prayer warrior and I spent time in warfare for his health. We used the keys of binding, loosing and knowledge that were given to us by divine revelation to destroy power of the spirits of infirmity and death. We declared his strength, healing and restoration through the power of the blood of Jesus Christ and the authority that He has given to us to use His name.

Within a few days, I received a text message stating that his deliverance was realized. Oh, the power of God is real! He will deliver his saints in the time of trouble, but we must stay connected in prayer. This minister's experience is become an eye opener even for myself. Sometimes our zeal to help others may lack the wisdom of God. We need to be very careful and move only in the timing and anointing of God. Although God gives us gifts for the needs of the body of Christ, and He gives the anointing to empower those gifts; when the anointing lifts and we continue to minister, we begin to operate in the gifts rather than the power of God. It is the anointing that energizes and educates in the things of God in addition to destroying all yokes of bondage and protecting those who minister. Oftentimes there are many unmet needs in a group and those who are seeking divine intervention for their situations may wish the minister prolongs the administration of his gift until they are helped. However, we ought to be wise for there is a time to minister and a time to wait on God. Jesus was anointed, but He did not heal all the sick or the needy around him. He knew when to take rest. We must do the same. We ought to pray for healthy balances so as not to grieve the Holy Spirit nor become burned out, for in neither condition are we any good to those in need of us.

Ministering Provision to Others

God is amazing. I awoke one morning and felt a need to just praise God for who He is and His goodness to me. That morning I said. "Today I am not asking for anything; I just want to praise you, Lord!"

While at work I had an accident with my watch. I thought about it, the potential for having to ship it and the questionable cost of repair. Then I thought: "You know what; I am not going to worry about it. I can see the time on the computer that I am using and when I am in my car, there is a clock that works". I described my situation in passing to a co-worker and continued working.

About two hours later a Christian friend of mine visited me at work. She brought me some lunch. Upon greeting her, she said: "I was at home when the Holy Spirit impressed on me to drop by to see you, so I have brought you a little light lunch." "How thoughtful of you!" I responded, "Please sit down." I proceeded to thank her for her generosity and showed her my ruined watch in conversation. In response she opened her hand bag and presented me a beautiful watch. "You can have this one." She said, and gave me the watch. I was utterly surprised. "I have four watches". She continued so "You can have this one." How great is our God! He is always on time - Hallelujah! In less than three hours God met my need for a watch. I used the event as a testimony to my co-workers, who were very amazed, especially the worker whom I had told earlier about the accident with my original watch.

A Prayer of Commission

Father we are excited with the miracles and answers to prayer that you often give to us. As we do your Kingdom work, please help us to always depend on you and not learn to our own understanding. Grant to us the strength, courage and wisdom we need and help us to always recognize your anointing and direction. Thank you, Father for being always there for us as provision and protection when we minister. Show us the things we need to know and we will be careful to obey you. Grant us your peace and victory in Jesus' name. Amen.

Chapter 8

Ministering to the Wounded Spirit

As we journey through life, there are many ups and down, joys and sorrows, trials, temptations, confrontations, sufferings, disappointments, victories and occasions for defeat. As Christians, we enjoy the good times, the mountain-top experiences of success and achievements, but are not exempt from the valleys of emotional and physical pain. We sometimes suffer in our relational experiences with others in the Body of Christ, the market places and our home. We are constantly in some kind of warring in this life. Suffering is a part of the believer's experience in the Christian walk, but when Christians suffer, may it be 'for righteousness' sake, for *"If we endure, we will reign with Him"*. (2Tim. 2:12a)

When the enemy attacks, he often cuts to the very core of your being, the heart. His goal is to destroy your joy, your worship of the Father and to sap your spiritual strength. He wounds your spirit and that can be devastating. King Solomon recognized this in his writing in the book of Proverbs in this saying. *"A crushed spirit, who can bear?"* (Prov. 18:14 NIV)

Satan uses people and circumstances to implement these schemes. Some assaults come from the Body of Christ through gossiping, false accusations, social cliques and prejudice. Damage can be done through spiritual wickedness in high places. The Holy Spirit, however, has placed within the body of Christ, anointed human vessels to be used in bringing healing, deliverance and restoration to the bruised, oppressed, depressed, insecure and fallen. God has a special purpose for every soul, and that purpose must prevail against the enemy's plans. The prophet Jeremiah pens it this way.

"For I know the thoughts and plans that I have for you, says the Lord. Thoughts and plans for welfare and peace and not for evil, to give you hope in your final outcome." (Jere. 29:11 AMP)

As one ministers to the wounded the focus is to bring Glory to Jesus at all costs. One needs to be prepared to go the extra mile with no hope for reward save that of knowing that the will of God is being done. That extra mile often takes sacrifice that moves that individual from his or her zone of comfort. The victim may have physical and emotional scars. The story in the Bible of the Good Samaritan who ministered to the wounded traveler on the Jericho road is a great model to consider. The Good Samaritan was not too busy to stop and show compassion to someone who was lying by the wayside wounded. He approached the individual, bound up the wounds, poured in oil and wine; set him own his own animal, brought him to an inn for additional care of paying the innkeeper to continue caring for the wounded man. Meanwhile, the ritualistic priest and Levite merely looked at the disabled traveler and passed by on the other side of the road.

When Believers Wound Each Other

Sometime ago, I was resting at home with the ugly symptoms of the influenza. A call came in from a spirit-filled adult. We will call her Sarah. She is a choir member in good standing at the church she worships weekly. However, she repeatedly encountered an insensitive tone and style of communication from another member – we will call John. Sarah never confronted John, but was at the point of wanting to quit participating in the church choir because of her unpleasant interactions with John. Her hurt crested and she was ready to take action.

As I listened, I quietly sought the Holy Spirit's insight and guidance and how to respond. What would Jesus do? I thought. I began by expressing my concern for her lack of peace and her general welfare. I asked a few questions to get Sarah to think and to communicate her real reason for being in the choir. She acknowledged a covenant she had made with God years ago. She wanted to be used for His glory in singing. Our brief discussion led Sarah to recognize how much she had neglected praying for the choir as a group as well as her interaction with John. We spoke of how God at times allows discomfort for "good" people to get their attention. God works in us in accordance with His good pleasure both to will, and to do, as He pleases. Not everyone gets a 'burning bush' experience like Moses, but God will stir us up when we are too much at ease in Zion.

I discussed with her an incident that occurred in the early church when, the apostles were spending all their time in Jerusalem, after the Pentecost experience in Acts 2. They hesitated in obeying the commission to spread the gospel from Jerusalem, to Judea, Samaria, and the utmost part of the earth. God allowed persecution to arise in Jerusalem to scatter the apostles to spread of the gospel. Sarah understood the analogy and realized that it was possible that God wanted more from her. We considered what the word of God had to say concerning handling offenses in Galatians 6. After discussing the power of forgiveness as a pre-requisite to releasing God's grace, we agreed in prayer for God's resolution.

A week later, I made a follow-up call simply to check her emotional well being. Sarah had a praise report. She was unable to return to choir practice because she was ill. However, when she notified the choir of her absence, the group prayed for her health. At the close of their meeting, who should call? You possibly guessed right. It was John! He wanted to know of her health and to ask her forgiveness for his unkind treatments towards her. Isn't God awesome? The Lord certainly got the glory! Praise God! Hallelujah! The enemy was defeated. Sarah has since then become more involved in intercessory ministry for the needs of the choir as well as the body of Christ.

When Wounded in the Market Place

A second illustration involves a young Christian whom I will name Tiffany. She was fresh out of the university and Holy Ghost filled. She had accepted employment out of the state of her residence. Her horrors began with her disillusionment between her perceived expectations and the realities she countenanced on the market place. It was not long before she felt somewhat betrayed, isolated and sense trapped for she had signed a contract in the recruitment phase of her employment. She had prayed about the decision to accept the position. She felt stressed, insecure, frustrated and disappointed. Her personal pride and enthusiasm were hurt. She was vulnerable, a wounded person. In a sense, she was also angry with God. Why was this happening to her? Did she not pray? Gradually the situation became more overwhelming and she needed help badly. She needed a miracle.

I prayed continually for divine wisdom in nurturing her spirit. She needed love, assurance, hope and deliverance. She was depressed. The Lord led me to take the position of warfare for this young woman. To bind the demonic force that was attacking her mind. At one point I engaged another saint to agree with me in prayer and warfare for her health, and deliverance. I would confess the word over Tiffany's life and circumstances. In one of the telephone meetings we spoke of Job's trouble and how God eventually delivered Job after a time; how when things seemed at their worst Job changed his position and worshipped God (Job 1:20).

However, Tiffany was angry with God and her spirit was not free to worship Him. Her faith in Him was severely tested, and she could not get a prayer through. My strategy involved reading the word in her hearing especially Psalms 46 and 91. I began to fast for her situation and agreed in prayer for a miracle of deliverance that would bring glory to God and destroy Satan's work. At that point, my prayer partner and I were not depending on Tiffany's faith, but rather on the greatness and bigness of our God. We stood on His promises and remembered past victories we experienced as a result of prayer. Within a couple of months, the Lord moved on the circumstances and opened a door for a change in employment; but Tiffany had to deal with the breech of contract and paid a fine.

The new job was different and manageable. Tiffany accepted the change, but still struggled with her worship. She needed more healing. In our conversations I would talk about the love of God, His mercy and grace and how we needed to learn to give praise and worship to God as a strategy until her emotional health was restored. I would sing a familiar chorus and encouraged her to join. Tiffany would not for she said she could not. No tune would come from her lips. She said that she had not sung a song in at least nine months. I was stunned. I kept encouraging her, but she did not sing that night. I went back into fasting and prayer for her deliverance.

Our next meeting, we read scriptures that exposed how crafty Satan was and his strategies. We emphasized what Jesus has done and the tools He has given us for victory. The conversation and the anointing of the Holy Spirit led her to resist the Devil by submitting to God, to repent, to let go of her hurt and embrace God who was waiting to heal her. God gave us His favor that session. She wept, repented and God showed His mercy. If only we can understand how to deal with sufferings and learn to trust in Jesus. The word teaches that what the enemy intends for evil, God can turn round and let it be for our good. (Rom. 8: 28).

Singing to God did not happen during that encounter, but the work had begun. By the next two sessions, the voice was returning to sing though a bit choppy at first. Today Tiffany has been restored, participates in a church where she fellowships with other friends and believers. She is a happier person. Her confidence in God returned. She has since done extra course work, changed careers and is joyfully serving the Lord in the market place. Oh! The goodness, the unfathomable love and mercy of God; Oh! The wisdom and power He gives as He uses vessels that are surrendered to Him to bring about the healing, deliverance and restoration of others.

Let me encourage you as a reader, if you identify with any of the content of this chapter, there is help for you in God. He loves you, more than you can ever imagine and regardless of your emotional state. He created you in His image and for His glory. He sees the smallest sparrow fall, and it never goes unnoticed at His feet, much more you. He sees you and knows the depth of your hurt. He wants to help you, to forgive you, to heal, and restore your joy. Call on the name of Jesus, cry out to Him for help, do not withhold your true feelings neither resist those whom He sends to your aid. In many instances we find we cannot do it alone, we need the assistance of others. May He put someone in your life that you can trust as you release your pain to the Lord.

A Prayer of Healing for the Wounded

Father thank you for your goodness and tender mercies that are available to us, because of who you are. Thank you that there is nothing too hard for you to do and that you are fully acquainted with all our ways and our needs. Help us to acknowledge you on the mountain top and in the valleys of life dear Father, for you are ever with us and want to bring us into your purpose and plan for living. As we come to you at this time, we lay all hurts, disappointments, and failure at your feet. We forgive those who have offended us and ask that you heal us physically, emotional and spiritually. In you are life, joy and peace. We worship you now and thank you in Jesus' Name. Amen.

Chapter 9

Responding to Hindrances in Ministry

"Thanks be to God who gives us the victory through our Lord Jesus Christ. Therefore, my brethren, stand firm.
Let nothing move you. Always give yourselves fully to the work of the Lord, because you know that your labor in the Lord is not in vain."
1 Cor. 15:57, 58 (NIV)

Ministry involves direct interface with Satan. Ministers are soldiers in God's army. In the battle to demolish satanic strongholds over victims' lives, to liberate minds, to heal diseases, to restore hope and salvation to the disenfranchised, kingdom workers suffer attacks and are sometimes vulnerable to Satan's schemes that are geared towards hindering effectiveness in ministry.

Here are some of the ways Satan presents his attacks:

Busyness

The adversary seeks to overwhelm you with the needs of others, to wear you down with activities and good works that are not necessarily God appointments for you at that time. You can become a people pleaser and miss your focus on God.

Have you ever tried to lay aside a special time for you and God only to find you are constantly being interrupted with telephone calls? They seem to come from the most unusual sources and sometimes by yielding to these requests you are seduced into participating in activities that totally consume your time, energy and fellowship with God. It's very difficult to truly focus and understand God's counsel when you are exhausted and drained. Daniel puts it this way: *'And (Satan) shall wear out the saints of the most High.'* Dan. 7:25 (AMP)

In order to defeat this tactic, we must know who we are in God and ask for His daily wisdom. Wisdom is the ability to know the right thing to do, at the right time for the maximum benefit. True wisdom comes from God and is peaceful. God desires us all to walk in wisdom and His holy fear. James tells us: *"If any of you lacks wisdom, he should ask God who gives generously to all, without finding fault and it shall be given to him."* (James 1:5 NIV) It is better to spend some time in diligent pursuit of God's wisdom than to make hasty decisions and be in error for which you will have regrets later on.

> *"Know that wisdom is sweet to your soul; if you find it, there is a future hope for you; and your hope will not be cut off."* Prov. 24:14 (NIV)

God's promises are true and abide forever, so grasp what He is saying in His word.

Likewise, we must follow Jesus' model while He was on earth. When it was time for Jesus to commune with His Father, He left everyone and everything. He separated Himself for an uninterrupted fellowship time with God. We must do the same for we constantly need the strength, power, revelation, wisdom and guidance of the Holy Spirit in our service to others. Those spiritual tools will only be granted when we spend quality time in God's presence. Whatever God tells you to do, be sure to obey and execute it in Jesus' name. We may become unpopular to some but we'll win over the Devil. We will not be burned out but rather be filled with grace, power and the Glory of God will rest upon us. We ought not to be afraid for God is with us even unto the end of this world. You and I are to experience victory for the sake of the name of Christ.

Distraction

Distraction is a Satanic tactic to delay, hinder and frustrate our plans. Distractions ignite an inner struggle to be faithful in doing the will of God and to satisfy the desires of the flesh. The heart is willing but the strongest temptations usually come at the time of our weakest moments which may be when we are feeling tired, lonely, hurt or frustrated. Sometimes we are overcome by them. We procrastinate on the things we aught to do, or are disobedient and find ourselves out of the will of God. Paul understood this for he included this statement in a letter to the Church in Rome.

"I know that nothing good lives in me, that is, in my sinful nature. For I have the desire to do what is good, but I cannot carry it out. For what I do is not the good I want to do; no, the evil that I do not want to do - this I keep on doing. Now if I do what I do not want to do, it is not longer I who do it, but it is sin living in me that does it....What a wretched man I am! Who will rescue me from this body of death? Thanks be to God, through Jesus Christ our Lord."
Rom. 7:18-20, 24, 25 (NIV)

We all know various sources and elements of distractions. They may be any of the following: television, computer, telephone, family problems, and job-related issues, busyness, and health concerns. God's plan for us is victory. In Him there is no defeat. Paul gave the church at Ephesus a strategy. He told the believers to wear the whole armor that God has tailor made for each one of them; that counsel is good for us today.

Procrastination

Procrastination comes to derail our mission focus. It is the thief of time. It is often very subtle in its operation and is destructive. It produces stress, leads to frustration and deception. I believe some spiritual correction that believers experience is the consequence of delayed obedience which is disobedience, which is a key tactic of Satan. Sometimes the enemy will use whatever tricks he can to frustrate and derail our plans. Many of us can identify with procrastination. This can be a serious matter, for when that spirit is operating in our lives; we can miss out on many blessings. Delay can be dangerous.

Paul writes:

"Be very careful, then, how you live – not as unwise but as wise,
Making the most of every opportunity, because the days are evil.
Therefore do not be foolish, but understand what the Lord's will is."
Ephe. 5:15-17 (NIV)

Disobedience

Sometimes disobedience can bring physical death. There is a story found in I Kings 13 that tells of a young prophet from Judah whom God sent to Bethel to expose King Jeroboam's sins while the king stood making an offering at the altar. God gave the prophet specific instructions. The king was offended and tried to assault the prophet. God demonstrated His power and sovereign authority in the prophet by causing the king's hand to shrivel up. The king had to humble himself and ask the young prophet to intercede to God for his healing, which God honored. Then the King invited the young prophet to dine at his residence. The young prophet refused the king's meal, being forewarned of God and he left to return to Judah. However, the enemy used an older prophet who had failed in his duty to address King Jeroboam's sins, to persuade the younger prophet with lying words, to return and eat at the older prophet's home. The younger prophet being seduced accepted the offer. That disobedience caused the younger prophet his life. For, while he ate, the older prophet revealed how he had tricked him into disobeying God which would cost him his life. Saddened, the younger prophet resumed his journey but was killed by a lion as he left the city.

When God speaks, God honors His word above his name. (Ps. 138:2) He expects obedience, for His word will not return to Him void, but will accomplish the purpose for which it was sent. (Is. 52:11). Make every effort to obey God's entire counsel with immediacy. He will provide a way of escape as we depend on Him. When in doubt worship Him, then be still and wait before Him. It is better to be safe than to be sorry.

Identifying the Hindrances

The following is a testimony of how God uses his ministers to counteract a Satanic distraction. Not long ago, a friend of mine testified of how the Lord used her in ministering to a needy person. We will call her Joyce. Joyce is an usher in her church. One Sunday a visitor brought a small child along with her to worship. Instead of using the nursery, she kept her child with her. As the sermon was being delivered the child became restless and noisy - affecting the other worshippers' ability to clearly hear the message. Joyce beckoned the mother to take the child to a more secluded area that would minimize the noise. Reluctantly, the mom obeyed. She apparently wanted to be in the service. She needed a blessing.

The Holy Spirit then spoke to Joyce to go and minister to the mother. The visitor wept as the Holy Spirit sensitized Joyce regarding the visitor's needs. Soon the Lord sent along one of the administrative members of staff who readily befriended the visitor. They exchanged telephone numbers with each other for further follow up and Joyce also gave the visitor the necessary information so that she could participate (if she desired) in the weekly prayer sessions at the Church for her continued support. The mother was very satisfied. Her feeling of anguish in having to leave the sanctuary to attend to her child, turned out to be an opportunity for God to provide for her spiritual needs to be met. So many times we encounter difficulties. It seems like we are facing contrary winds in life; but God can turn our disappointments into blessings, for He sees our needs and satisfies them according to His riches in glory, for He is Jehovah Jireh. What the enemy intends for evil, God will turn it for good; and that is what He did for the visitor and her child that Sunday. The secret is to pray, release the situation to Jesus and believe He will work it out. Keep your focus on Him and His promises. Seek to ponder on His nature and any past victories that He has given you. Have great expectations of Him, for He will do it again. Hold on to your faith in the tough times. It is said that the darkest hour of the night is just before the dawn of day, but the daylight will appear.

Understanding therefore, that the enemy's plan is to steal one's joy, frustrate one's will and knowing that God is more powerful than the Devil, that it is God's plan which must prevail and not Satan's, let us examine some strategies that we can use to overcome the Devil's schemes.

Goal Setting With Accountability to Counteract Obstacles

Prayerfully establish goals in whatever you are hoping to accomplish, a plan of action with time lines. Where there isn't a plan, it is easy to drift from focus. Establish priorities. We must ask the Lord to show us how to distinguish between what is lawful versus that which is expedient. Whatever hinders us from advancing our purpose should be evaluated and severed. We need to establish bench marks and periodically reflect on our progress. It is also important to have frequent spiritual check ups. These happen through set periods of prayer and worship. Don't be anxious to leave God's presence, but wait on Him for council. Whatever He births into your spirit is to be acted upon. To obey is better than sacrifice and those who wait upon the Lord, He renews their strength, to mount up with wings like eagles, to run and not be weary, to walk and not faint.

We need someone with whom to establish accountability. This helps to keep us focused as we fulfill our responsibilities. That person should be a prayer warrior who intercedes and keeps both you and your project covered with constant prayer. *"The prayer of a righteous man is powerful and effective."* James 5:16 (NIV)

Resetting God as the Center When Discouraged

A young man we will call John, shared with me a series of events in his life that made him feel emotionally entrapped within, discouraged and depressed. He had made a few moves in life, none of which gratified his needs, and at the time of our conversation was in the process of seeking a job and career change. He had twice failed the qualifying exam for the new career. He had only one more chance left. His anxiety was high, he was worried, felt stressed, and he was very aware that any failure would disappoint his parents and hurt his pride. He needed to be encouraged. Our discussion led him to reflect on his past victories, and how God blessed him then, and how God wanted to do it again, for there is no failure in God. However, in order to win John needed to change his way of thinking and to position him for the blessing. How could he do that?

He began with putting back God at the center of his life and plans. He acknowledged God as the author and finisher of his faith; as having plans for his life; plans to prosper him and to bring him to His desired will. During our time together, John read several scriptures from the word of God that were relevant to his situation. In them, he saw the love of God for him and that God would not withhold any good thing from those who walked uprightly before Him.

We identified and took authority over the spirit of discouragement, fear of failure and depression; and bound them in Jesus' name. We released the spirit of peace, soundness of mind and victory through faith in Jesus. The young man felt relieved. His countenance changed. God had done something special for him. He had a new attitude. The Lord began to show him how and what to study so that one month later, he passed the exam and began his new employment. Hallelujah! Great is the Lord and marvelous are His works!

Discouragement is a weapon Satan uses to decrease an individual's courage and hope. He seeks to ruin his or her confidence, faith and reliance on God. The Devil has one ultimate goal and that is to get that person to abort his or her dreams. Discouragement brings the soul into bondage. That is why we must not give it a foot hold in our minds. That spirit often comes through sad news, failed attempts and disappointments. It is indiscriminate in its attacks. Leaders and laymen alike are all vulnerable. Here are two examples from God's word:

When the children of Israel came to the border of Canaan, they became discouraged with the assessment in the report referring to the new land the Lord had given to them. This is what they said:

"Where can we go up? Our brethren have discouraged our hearts, saying, the people are greater and taller then we; the cities are great and fortified up to heaven; moreover we have seen the sons of the Anakim there." Deut. 1:28 (NKJV)

Discouragement brings emotional paralysis. The children of Israel had forgotten the mighty deliverances they experienced at the hand of God as they journeyed in the wilderness. They were short-sighted in seeing God's protection and provision. It seemed they were disregarding God's promise to them in His word that Moses had given to them when he turned over the leadership to Joshua.

"And Moses summoned Joshua, and said to him in the presence of all Israel, be strong, and courageous, for thou must go with the people into the land that the Lord swore to their fore-fathers to give them; and you must divide it among them as their inheritance. The Lord himself goes before you; he will never leave you

nor forsake you. Do not be afraid; do not be discouraged." Deut. 31; 7, 8 (NIV)

When our plans fall apart even kings can become discouraged. King David, who is referred to in the scriptures as, *"a man after God's own heart"* is no exception. One of King David's source's of discouragement stemmed from his error in judgment. The nation of Israel was at war with its neighbors the Amorites and soon afterwards, the Philistines. David was victorious in all the battles thus far, for God was with Him. David depended on God. Then, there was the battle against the Philistines and David decided to take a census so that he could determine more accurately the strength of his army against the Philistines. He ordered Joab, one of his top generals, to count the Israelites from Beersheba to Dan. He demanded this against the godly counsel offered to him.

David's action had devastating consequences that utterly discouraged him. Taking the census was an indication that David was beginning to place confidence more in the number of his troops than in the power of God. As a result, God allowed David to choose one of three forms of punishment. He could select either three years of famine, or three months of defeat by his enemies, or three days, with the sword of the Lord, when the Angel of the Lord would destroy the children of Israel with a plague. David accepted the final option and God punished David by sending a pestilence upon Israel that took the lives of seventy thousand men. 1 Chron. 21:14 (AMP).

David along with the elders repented in sackcloth. He asked God to let the punishment be put on him and his household instead the entire nation of Israel, for it was the sin of one man and not the entire nation. God answered by allowing David to purchase an area of land at full price to establish an altar to God where he offered sacrifices in atonement for the sin that he had committed. The entire story can be found in 1 Chronicles chapters 21 and 22.

How shall one defeat the spirit of discouragement? The goal is to regain hope, joy, and peace with God, to challenge the individual to move forward with restored confidence in God. First we need to trace the cause of discouragement. Get the facts straight. One must not simply work on assumptions, for Satan is known as the accuser of the brethren. Where we are dealing with emotions, imagination, pride, and error we are to use the *logos* word to reveal truth to the victim and dispel all errors.

Sometimes discouragement comes from disobedience to God. Sometimes we are self-willed, overwhelmed, and have suffered disappointments and defeat. We ought to immediately seek the Lord, confess and repent of our actions. He is forgiving and merciful. His love endures forever. This gets rid of guilt.

> *"If we confess our sins, he is faithful and just and will forgive us our sins and purify us from all unrighteousness"*. 1 Jn 1:9 (NIV)

Get back into the word. We overcome through the blood of Jesus and the word of our testimony. Engage a prayer partner to assist you in identifying and pulling down all of Satan's lies. We need our minds to be renewed by the word of God. The Bible records that we are to:

> *"Cast down arguments and every high thing that exalts itself against the knowledge of God bringing every thought into captivity, to the obedience of Chris, and being ready to punish all disobedience when your obedience is fulfilled."* Cor. 10:5 (NKJV)

Often times, it helps to write down one's feelings. Then write out what the word of God says relative to that emotion. Recite, receive and accept what God says in His word. For example, the enemy tries to deceive people into thinking that God has left them. The truth is in the word that states: *"Never will I leave you; never will I forsake you"*. Heb.13:5 (NIV)

Satan says, "You are just wasting your time, and nothing good will come of your efforts." The word says: *"In all things God works for the good of those who love him, who have been called according to His purpose."* Rom. 8:28 (NIV)

The enemy says, "People hurt you, all they do is hurt you and they will surely keep on hurting you". The word says:

> *"We do not wrestle against flesh and blood, but against principalities, against powers, against the rulers of darkness of this age against spiritual hosts of wickedness in heavenly places. Therefore, take the whole armor of God, that you might be able to withstand in the evil day, and having done all, to stand."* Ephe. 6:12 (NKJV)

Satan says, "God is sure punishing you, can't you see?" The word says:

> *"My son, do not despise the chastening of the Lord, nor be discouraged when you are rebuked by Him; for whom the Lord loves, He chastens, and scourges every son whom He receives."* Heb.12:6 (NKJV)

Satan says, "You are weak and a failure, your strength is gone, you won't make it." God's word declares:

> *"My grace is sufficient for you, for my power is made perfect in weakness."* 2 Cor.12:9 (NIV)

"It is not my might, nor by power, but by My Spirit, says the Lord Almighty". Zech. 4:6 (NKJV)

The believer needs to pray and release to God all the emotions, to forgive him or herself and others who might have caused hurt or spiritual pain. Be sure to tell the Lord of your will to accept only what He says in His word about you.

Maintain self encouragement by reading various psalms. They are excellent for all types of needs. As you read and meditate, see yourself being helped, and pray the psalm back to the Lord in acknowledgment of His meeting your needs. Some favorites among the Psalms are: Psalms 23, 42, 63, 91 and 149.

The Word of God also admonishes us to put on the garment of praise for the spirit of heaviness. We are to lift up our voices and sing unto the Lord! Praise Him! Magnify Him! And lift Him up! Give the sacrifice of praise to God! For praise glorifies Him. When the Glory of the Lord comes upon those who praise Him, He releases joy, healing, deliverance and restoration. Offer the sacrifice of praise the fruit of our lips giving Him thanks. Praise brings deliverance. Seek to pray in tongues to help build up our renewed faith and courage in God. He will restore your soul's peace, joy and happiness.

Standing against Confusion

Have you ever planned your day's activity only to discover that you have misplaced your important keys for the home and car? Isn't it worrisome, time consuming and self condemning when you are in a hurry and you have not a clue where to find them? That is another way that the enemy attacks the mind. He releases the spirit of confusion and anxiety, but God is our deliverer. I have had that experience.

Sometime ago, I kept the keys to my car, home, alarm system, work and the church on the same bunch. Habitually there was one location that I would hang those keys in my home, for ready use as needed. Interestingly one morning, that did not happen. I had used them outdoor in my backyard the previous day and assumed that I had replaced them to the usual spot. It was a busy morning. I was rushing to accomplish a few things before going to work. When time came for me to use the keys, they were no where to be found indoors. I tried hastily to re-trace the activities I had done. I just could not imagine where they could have been. I prayed, but was too anxious to focus on what the Lord was saying. Only thing I was certain of was that I had used them that morning. By then, I was late for work. I prayed and placed my home under the Blood of Jesus. I asked his angelic protection over the premises and location of the keys. I used a second set of keys for the car and garage to get to work. I was embarrassed but was able to access my office with a second set of office keys that was required to remain at the work site.

That day I struggled in my emotions. Why did this happen to me? However, I am at work. I must be pleasant, and be at peace so that I may serve others with the peace that God gives. Our mood impacts our behavior. I took a few minutes to focus on God and the word that tells us to put on the whole armor of God to be able to withstand the wiles of the devil. I began to confess the word and to plead the Blood of Jesus over my mind. I confessed that I have the mind of Christ and that angels were on assignment keeping and protecting my home and keys. I embraced the promise that God will keep me in perfect peace, if I keep my mind on Him. (Is. 26:3). The day went well at work. I joined my exercise program after work. It was time to get home and resume the search.

I looked indoors and did not find those keys. By then it was dark and I was becoming anxious. Then a Christian friend called and upon hearing my story, she prayed God's peace and revelation be given to me. I slept that night and dreamed that the keys were found. Awaking the next morning the Holy Spirit impressed the words "The donkeys have been found" (1 Sam. 30:1). I thanked Him, and proceeded to read the entire story of Saul and the missing donkeys. I discovered that God had a greater plan for Saul, who unknowingly, was to meet Samuel to be anointed to become the king of Israel. The loss of the donkeys was a temporary measure to bring Saul into God's greater plan. I sought the Lord for revelation and prayed His will be done. Then He led me outdoors and showed me the keys in my backyard. He protected them. There was no rain as was forecasted for that night, only the dampness from the dew. The electronics in them worked perfectly. Oh! How I felt relieved. To God be the glory!

In spite of that victory my spiritual antenna was raised. I needed to know the purpose in this whole trial and the essence of the dream. For, Saul had set out to find donkeys but he returned with donkeys plus the anointing for kingship later. I maintained my thanksgiving and worship focus. Later that day the Holy Spirit led me to connect with a spiritual leader regarding an important e-mail. I was awaiting a reply to a request that up until then was not granted, and I assumed might have been over looked or forgotten. That day providentially we met, and I heard the Spirit say, "Go now and speak to the leader". I obeyed hardly knowing what to say, but began with the salutation. The Lord guided the conversation that led me to make mention of the e-mail. I then learned that he had not received my communication and the situation was quickly resolved. It was amazing how God exposed and destroyed the works of Satan whose strategy was to frustrate the plans for the ministry.

We need to know the Lord, and that trials come to make us strong and wise. Remember God is with us, and all things will work for the greater good when God is in it. Hold on to

Jesus! Hold on to His promises and His word, and He will surely bring you out. He restores the soul. I am a witness.

A Prayer for Freedom to Minister

Thank you for the opportunity to bring every emotion and every care to the cross, knowing that you care for us. Forgive us for the times when we have focused on our situations and circumstances, more so than on your mighty power and your grace. Grant us the understanding and wisdom to put the enemy under our feet and to conquer every obstacle and hindrance to your work in us, for us and through us. We thank you for the weapons of our warfare that you have given to us in your word to make us over comers in this life. We will ever seek to praise your glorious name. Thank you for victory in Jesus' name. Amen.

Chapter 10

Maintaining your Spiritual House

"Thou therefore my son, be strong in the grace that is in Christ Jesus." 2Tim. 2:1 (NKJV)

Many ministers live in a house or parsonage that is provided by their congregation while they serve that congregation. Believers are living stones that collectively constitute a spiritual house or parsonage of sorts – a place of provision and shelter for kingdom ministry. The word of God is the foundation of that house and Jesus is the chief corner stone. In a natural house, the building blocks are held together with mortar and cement. The structure is frequently examined for damages from storms, winds, floods, earthquakes, general use and misuse. Repairs reinforce, restore and even to up-grade the structure entirely.

Spiritually speaking, believers are kept by the power of God, and unified with each other by the Holy Spirit. It is fascinating how the Holy Spirit dwells in each believer. His body is the temple of God, and is a stone in the spiritual house. Your personal care of your life in Christ Jesus reflects the quality of stone that you contribute to the parsonage.

What are you? Are you granite, marble, limestone or chalk?

The anointing of God, prayer and *agape* love are the glue that binds and sustains strength in the building. How do we go about doing this?

The bible says that we are to work out our personal salvation with fear and trembling. That means we must cultivate and practice personal discipline, dedication and commitment to grow in God's word and to submit in obedience to Him. We also must not forget to assemble ourselves together with others in the Body of Christ. Some churches provide such opportunities in home small groups in addition to times of corporate prayer and other meetings.

Iron sharpens iron. When we study the word together, we edify one another. God gives revelations and empowerment to the hearers to be able to apply the principles for daily living. As we testify and lift up Jesus, the Father gets glory; and that is His will for us. Testimonies enlighten others, give them hope and challenge their faith in God, knowing that God brought others through victoriously, and is able to do the same for them as well. It is just a matter of time and holding on to their faith. Every testimony releases the Holy Spirit to do a similar thing for someone else. This is a vital part of ministry one to another. For it is the Holy Spirit that testifies of Jesus in you and Jesus says: *"If I be lifted up from the earth, I will draw all peoples to Myself."* Jn 12:32 (NKJV)

In the corporate assembly believers also receive the ministry of the word with sometimes miracles of healing and deliverances. *"He sent His word and healed them"*. Ps. 107:20 (NKJV). It is also true that in the corporate worship, as we minister to the Father extolling Him, honoring and praising Him, God rebuilds and restores any spiritually broken walls. He energizes our spirit and gives us the grace to recover from lost focus. He even shows us how, what and when if you are being deceived.

We are to guard against the tricks of Satan. He knows exactly how to tempt us to overspend our budgets and keep us in financial bondage; how to cause us to work two and three jobs over prolonged periods that deprive us of enjoying family availability, communication and unity. He is skilled at turning discussions into arguments because of low tolerance for each other, exhaustion from insufficient rest, improper diet and physical body maintenance. He is crafty at bringing about emotional deprivation in families. Everyone becomes too busy for each other; the television, computer games and chat rooms, cell phone and telephones replace the human touch and concerns. Satan gets a field day when he sees us all stressed out with unfinished deadlines for over committed responsibilities of our choosing, whether for personal fame or for social acceptance. During such times, our prayer and devotion time with the Father is minimized; Bible reading is limited to perhaps once day a week for a few minutes. Then even during those times, the mind is drifted everywhere, so that we fail to receive instructions and guidance from the word of God. When we get to Church, we often are overtaken by sleep, and so miss out on the messages the Spirit of God is sending to the church.

Do you identify with any part of the scenario just described? Then know assuredly that you are under the attack of the enemy. He begins with the gradual compromise of your time and commitment to God. Compromise is like termites in your spiritual house. If you overlook their presence and existence, they will destroy your building. When someone is too busy to pray, to spend with God in the word, then you are *too* busy. Every minister is exposed to Satan's tricks, so do not be ignorant of Satan's devices.

We can overcome through fasting, prayer meditating and obeying his word. Fasting brings the body and its appetites of lust, greed, covetousness, selfishness, self- will under the

Spirit's control. Paul says: "*I beat my body under, and make it my slave.*" 1Cor.9:27 (NIV). For, says he,

> "*We have an obligation – it is not to fulfill the sinful nature. For if you live according to that nature, you will die, but if by the Spirit you put to death the deeds concerning the body you will live. Because those who are led by the Spirit are the sons of God.*
> Rom. 8:12-14 (NIV)

God will reveal what the enemy is doing. He will show a way of escape and empower us to defeat Satan's plans. Get in the habit of scheduling some time for God. May be it is early in the morning or mid-day. Seek His face in prayer and the word. Ask Him to remove all hindrances to your focus and spiritual growth and to grant you His wisdom, knowledge, understanding and balance in life that you may be all He wants you to be. He honors sincere prayers. "*Everything that my heavenly Father has not planted shall be pulled up from the root.*" Matt 15:13 (NIV)

A Prayer for Spiritual Devotion

Heavenly Father I come to you in the name that is above all names, Jesus, the only name in which there is power to do exceedingly above and beyond all that I can ask or think. I admit my life often times seems winding out of your Spirit's control. I present to you my body, the faculties of my mind and spirit. Please forgive me for all my weaknesses and errors due to any distraction or miscalculation. Deliver me from all habits and indulgences that choke out quality time with you. Teach me how to budget my time and activities that enable me to be victorious over all the strategies of the devil. When I forget, please quicken my understanding, when I am tempted to do things my way, please renew my mind by you word that it may always be girded with your truths. I chose to be mindful to wear your whole armor and to apply the principles of the word in my life from this time forth in Jesus' mighty name. Amen.

Chapter 11

Exalting Jesus Everywhere

"You are the salt of the earth... You are the light of the world... Let your light shine before men, that they may see your good deeds and praise your Father in heaven." Matt. 5: 13a, 14a, 16 (NIV)

Over 2,000 ago, Jesus spoke to His disciples, and challenged them to be salt and light in the world. Salt is a powerful mineral, it prevents putrefaction and decay; but salt is useless until it is poured from its container and applied to the object of need. Christians are synonymous to salt. We bear the savor of Christ that the world needs. Millions are decaying in the dens of sin and ignorance. They are without hope, and will be eternally lost unless we release unto them the salt we possess. Light dispels darkness, ignorance and error. Jesus warned that light was not to be hidden but to be positioned to illuminate everything in its range. Collectively Christians are to shine like the constellation of stars in the heavens on a dark night. Individually each of us is to radiate light as a lighthouse that guides the ship in the ocean to the harbor of safety.

The light in each of us is the reflection of the image of the truth, love, grace and peace of our Lord and Savior Jesus

Christ. The light must shine. The reflection is magnified and Christ is revealed everywhere we go. Just think of how many individuals we meet in the many adventures we take, in the places we go and the activities in which we become engaged. Some even express their admiration for us; as they continually observe behaviors, attitudes, values and lifestyle. Some emulate us; some regard us as their heroes and mentors. They love to be in our company and the qualities we reflect shine as light on their path of need. Jesus wants us to display His glory in all the earth that souls will be drawn to Him and His Kingdom. Let us look at a few examples of how souls have been won for Jesus.

In the Parking Lot

Not long ago, I was a speaker at a Women's Convention. During the presentation I left some small articles in the custody of a friend with whom I had shared the breakfast table. The friend had to leave for work before the conclusion of the meeting, and mistakenly took the keys to my home and car with her. I was stranded. I wanted to get home. After connecting with her by telephone she agreed to have her husband return the keys. My car was the only one left in that parking lot on that sunny Saturday afternoon. I leaned on it and waited.

As the husband came and delivered the keys, he began to express some of his emotions, discomfort and frustration. I had met him a year before and had agreed with the family in prayer on the purchase of a second home as an investment property. I will name the husband Peter. He needed to release his feelings of disappointment, emotional pain and hurts. I remembered Peter saying that something had to give or he might either commit suicide or permanently walk away from his marriage and family. "I will sell that new property; I just want out of all this." He said and sighed.

"Wow"! I thought to myself. "Peter is very upset. Am I the last stop before he does some radical thing? Lord, teach me how to handle this situation. After all, this is a family that I know and love. The wife is Spirit-filled, and the husband believes in you." God gave me grace, a listening ear and wisdom to address the issue. We spent almost three hours in that parking lot, at the end of which, there was a turning point in Peter's life for the glory of God. The Lord enabled Peter to recognize some long standing wounds he entertained even before the marriage that needed to be addressed. As we spoke about Lordship in the home, attitudes, communication styles and family prayer, we were able to see how Satan was steadily infiltrating the marriage with a goal to wreck it. I told Peter that God loved the family so much that He convened our meeting that day to expose and destroy the plans of the enemy.

Peter needed the healing grace of God activated in his life. He knew that, he was led to recognize that except the Lord built the house, those who built, labored in vain. We discussed how God hated divorce, and wanted to heal the wounded heart, to lift up the forsaken, to deliver everyone that was brought into captivity by Satan. The first step to change was to acknowledge his need, and that the only true source of fulfillment for the rest of his life, was in Jesus. "Don't continue your focus on any right that you feel was violated," I remarked. "We are not dealing with flesh and blood. What we are dealing with are evil spirits that attack the mind through circumstances. We are not always right in our responses either, so let us give everything to Jesus to resolve."

"Today can be your turning point, Peter", I said. "God will do a new thing in you if you will let Him. Right now, the focus is on you and your personal relationship with Him. Before you can effectively deal with domestic and other situations you need Jesus to be Lord in your life. He will save you, heal you; strengthen you with His wisdom, understanding and power in your inner man. Are you willing to let Him into your life?"

Peter expressed his willingness and agreed with me in prayer. He was allowed to express and release his feelings to Jesus in that parking lot. We bound the spirits of anger, frustration, deception, depression and suicide in Jesus' name and released the spirit of forgiveness, peace, love and grace. I then led him through the sinner's prayer. Peter wept as he surrendered his life to salvation in Christ. The Lord surely did a miracle and saved him that moment. Praise the Lord! Peter said he felt as if a weight had been lifted from him. He had begun the new life in Jesus.

That night when the wife got home, she sensed a difference in her husband, one that brought her much joy. She called me and asked: "Mary what did you all do? My husband is a different man, I can hardly believe it. Tell me what happened?" "Just give the Lord the Praise and Glory!" I responded. "Your husband will tell you all about it in the fullness of time." Since then there has been such a positive change in the home. Peter started on a journey to know God in his word. He continued to be a diligent participant in a cell group that met weekly. We were teaching a series on the "Work of the Holy Spirit in the Believer's Life". Peter's work schedule made it difficult for him to be on time for the sessions, but he would show up anyway with his homework completed and whatever questions he accumulated during his studies. He was hunger for truth. He wanted more than 'hearing about God', he wanted the experience of the fullness of the anointing of God that comes through the infilling of the Holy Spirit.

> *"Blessed are those who hunger and thirst for righteousness: for they shall be filled."*
> Matt. 5: 6 (NKJV)

At the close of the session, I announced that we would be seeking for the infilling of the Holy Spirit's blessing the following week, and that we should prepare our vessels through prayer, repentance, and forgiveness of all whom we perceive have hurt us. We were also to confess any mistakes that we have made, and to forgive ourselves for those errors we have made, knowing that God forgives the penitent heart.

> *"Who shall ascend into the hill of the Lord? Who shall stand in his holy place? He that hath clean hands, and a pure heart; who has not lifted up his soul unto vanity, nor sworn deceitfully; he shall receive the blessing from the Lord, and righteousness from the God of his salvation."* Ps. 24:3, 4 (NKJV)

Both husband and wife attended the meeting. That evening Peter prepared himself and was on time for the session. In his testimony later, he confessed that he even fasted that day in anticipation of the blessing. Surely enough, that night as we assembled, prayed and began to worship the Lord with all our hearts, the Glory of the Lord came down in that home and God baptized Peter with the Holy Spirit. He experienced the manifestation with the speaking in tongues in less than fifteen minutes into the session. It was a most memorable night. There was so much joy and happiness in the meeting. Peter gave his testimony of how it all got started with the encounter in the parking lot; how he gave his life to Jesus and could hardly find words to express the joy that the Holy Spirit has deposited into him. No one else can bless us like Jesus can bless us. Isn't that awesome?

There are a few points we need to grasp from this example:

- Troubles in life come to draw us closer to our Savior and sometimes closer to our ministry assignment.
- The heart that seeks God truly will find Him. Be willing to surrender to God.
- God wants to heal, sustain and bless marriages.
- We are to be available to be used by God despite the circumstances.
- God convenes situations for His glory, and will allow all things to work together for good to those who love and fear Him and to bring glory to His name.

Since those meetings, I am proud to write that this family has been doing really well. They are now in business. They pray together, share together and are growing together. It is fascinating to note, that while writing this book, I received a call from the wife letting me know how God has been blessing the family and opening doors of opportunity for them. He has put an experienced Christian businessman in their path that will be mentoring them. What a God we serve!

Let us not give Satan credit when our plans are disrupted for God may be ordering our steps for His glory. Just praise and stay focused and see what happens. We are to take the name of Jesus with us, everywhere we go over land and sea. The good news of Jesus is to be spread to all nations, tribe and tongue. Whatever be your assignment I encourage you to get rid of all fear and shyness that we all suffer, at one time or another. If you are accepted great! If not, do not take it personally.

On the Phone

There are many members in my family who know about God, but have not met Him personally. The Lord has used me in encouraging their hearts over a number of years through a variety of ways. I tend to love to travel, and from time to time I have made several trips to London where most of them have lived over the years. A brother and two sisters have accepted Christ as their Savior but there are others yet outside the door of Salvation for which I believe God to draw them to receive His saving Grace in the fullness of time. One plants, the other waters, but it is God who gives the increase.

On my most recent trip to Europe, the Lord let me realize that He had ordained my travel time for His glory. He allowed me to witness Jesus to a French student, a Russian lady and a New York teenager on the planes I flew. The young teenager had just received her First Communion being Catholic and needed to know and accept that it is only through Jesus and not the Virgin Mary is as the way to the Father according to John 14:6.

God has allowed me to maintain follow up communication with the Russian lady. I send her materials and encourage her in bible reading and understanding the scriptures. She now attends a bible believing church in New York City. In London, no additional family members gave their hearts to the Lord, on that trip, but they respected my witness, and I thanked the Lord that at least the family where I stayed, listened and showed some interests in the truth of the scriptures. Rome was not built in a day and God will perfect that which He has started. I have hope for their salvation. There were times of fellowship, and even the blessing of an infant. I have learnt that since then, the parents have been attending a bible believing Church, and they too, I strongly believe, will be saved.

On the Street

Just as God can take us abroad to spread His kingdom, He can use us in our communities. It took a simple appointment, a morning's walk for God to save a young man. I was doing the periodic morning walk and praying in the neighborhood, when I met two teenagers walking with a dog in the opposite direction. "Hello, young men of valor! How are you today?" I asked. They appeared surprised, but I was very pleasant and engaged them in a short conversation. I explained what I meant in calling them 'young men of valor'. Then I asked, "Have you heard of the exciting youth program that is going on at our Church?" "I'm a member of another Church!" responded one of them.

"Great!" I replied. "How about you?" I asked the second young man. "I follow my friend sometimes to his Church." He answered. "That's good!" I said. "But tell me, do you know Jesus?" One said yes, while the other reserved his answer. They must have wondered what this lady is up to. The Lord taught me how to pleasantly engage them in a conversation that dealt with how Jesus had a special plan for their lives, including eternal life, so that after living in this life they would have the chance to live for ever with the Lord. I told them that God had a unique plan for each of their lives and how much God wanted them to know Him and to establish a permanent consistent relationship with them for each to receive the fullness of His blessings for his personal life. The Lord further allowed me to explain that going to church would help cultivate a relationship with God. "He wants to live in your hearts and be your Lord". I further explained that God was everywhere, and that His presence was with us even there in the street.

"Sometimes God sends people into our lives at the time when He wants us to respond if we believe in Him and the words spoken to us" I continued. After a short conversation, the unsaved youth surrendered his life to Christ in the street. They then asked my name and place of worship. I was glad to give them the address of the church and to let them know they were in the Kingdom of God and were free to get their parent's permission to attend any of the programs for the youths, including their worship and praise of God. They went their way and I continued my walk.

Who knows what God has in store for those two young men that He gave them a divine appointment for such a life changing event that day? It was the Holy Spirit who also impressed on me to take that route. I had often gone in the opposite direction. God's will surely prevailed for that young man's life that day. It is good and profitable to be led by the Holy Spirit. Someone always gets blessed.

In the Hospital

God will save people anywhere. This testimony tells of how He accomplished salvation in the life an ill person. The patient's wife had accepted Jesus as Savior in a crusade some years ago. The husband had not and was very strong-willed. When we first met before the illness and spoke about the Lord, he was defensive. He claimed that he went to church all the time and that was it. Sometime later, he became seriously ill and was hospitalized. I made a couple of trips to visit in the hospital a distance of over one hundred miles round trip from my home. Each visit I became more concerned about his salvation, but had not the courage to mention the topic. There were always other visitors and it just did not seem as if it was the right time. I would enquire about his condition, read his favorite scriptures, and say a prayer and journey back home. His prognosis was not good. I felt inwardly troubled. I prayed and asked the Lord to grant the patient life, and to allow me to present Christ and salvation to him. I had to leave the country for two weeks. During that interval of time, there was not a day I did not think of the patient and hoped that the Lord would spare his life in spite of the poor health prognosis that the doctor described.

Upon returning home, I enquired about the patient. He was alive, but with no improvement and was himself loosing hope. His medical team had transferred his care to another hospital that was closer, about fifteen miles from my home. I visited him there. He seemed glad to see me and to hear me continue to read the scriptures to him. Again he had others visitors at the time of my visit. Later as I got home, I fell to on my knees and prayed. I said:

> "Lord, you have laid this soul on my heart, please fix whatever needs to be fixed and give me the courage to do your will". Amen.

On my day of fasting I lifted up the patient before God. He gave me the assurance in the word: "[He] shall not die, but live and declare the Glory of God." That Sunday morning, after worship and praying at my home Church, I visited the hospital. The patient was alone. Praise God! The Lord anointed me to get straight to the point of his salvation. He allowed me to tell the patient that it was not God's will to call him home at that time, but it was His will to save his life if he would receive Jesus; that merely attending a church would not secure him a place in heaven, but salvation would.

Amazingly, there was no resistance. It was as if he had been waiting for me to initiate the step. I told him that one of the benefits of Salvation is healing for Jesus was wounded for our transgression, was bruised for our iniquity and by His stripes we were healed. I led through the scripture, the ABC's of salvation summarized below:

> A. All have sinned and come short of the glory of God. There is none righteous, no not one. The wages of sin is death, but the gift of God is Eternal life in Christ Jesus' Rom. 6:23 (NKJV)
> B. Believe on the Lord Jesus Christ and you shall be saved. For God so loved the world, that He gave His one and only Son, that whoever believes in

Him shall not perish, but have eternal life. For God did not send his Son into the world to condemn the world, but to save the world through Him. Whoever believes on Him is not condemned, but whoever does not believe, stands condemned already, because he has not believed in the name of God's one and only Son. (Jn 3:16-18) Most assuredly, I say unto you, he who believes on Me has eternal life. Jn. 6:47 (NKJV)

C. Confession with you mouth. "If you confess with your mouth, that Jesus is Lord and believe in your heart that God raised Him from the dead, you shall be saved. For it is with your heart you believe and are justified, and it is with your mouth that you confess and are saved. Rom. 10:9, 10 (NKJV)

We prayed and God blessed him with the miracle of salvation. I then encouraged and gave him the word from the Lord that he would not die, for God would surely raise him up. That was nothing short of a miracle. He had lost so much weight. His appetite was gone. He could not tolerate solids and God changed all of that. He was released from the hospital. Gradually his appetite returned. Now he is driving again and regaining the weight. He is attending his church, but with the difference. Isn't the Lord great! Hallelujah!

God's Mandate

Witnessing and serving in ministry is God's divine mandate for our lives. We can make a difference. Some are called to the mission field away from their homes and loved ones. Others find their ministry is in their very homes, among their children and loved ones. We minister in the lives we live, those we help to live, the words we speak and the things we do for the kingdom of God. Some are part of the five fold ministry to the Church. Others are intercessors, prayer warriors, exhorters, motivators and general helpers. They go where the Holy Spirit dictates. They serve who ever wills to receive them. They labor seeking no reward, save that of knowing that are doing God's will. They travel over land and sea. They speak the word; pray the word, testify the word; and the power of the witness changes lives by the Holy Spirit.

It's my prayer that you see yourself as a minister, and that the contents of this book help you to engage in the calling to fulfill your purpose and God's plan for your life.

A Prayer of Communion

Father I pray for the readers of this narrative. I thank you for giving them the courage to read this book. I pray that you will bless them indeed with all they will need to become effective ministers in your Kingdom. May you grant Salvation to the one who has not committed his life to you, may you fill each hungry soul with the knowledge, revelation, anointing and courage to step out of their boat into the main stream of ministering your Life, Word to those in need. Heavenly Father, by your Spirit and your word, many of us recognize that there is more you want from us than we are doing. Lord we often make excuses of being tired, ignorant and or busy; but Lord you have given unto us all that pertains to life and godliness. You have equipped up with the anointing of your presence and power. Stir our hearts with the concerns that you have for souls. We are your agents in the earth. Awake us from our lethargy, open our eyes to see that by the evidence of the signs of the time, you are soon to come back, and that we must be about our Father's business. Grant us the commitment and strength to labor until you return. I ask in Jesus' Name. Amen.